Beginner's Guide to Japanese Joinery

Jin Izuhara

Table of Contents

Introduction

Welcome to **A Beginner's Guide to Japanese Joinery.** Japanese carpentry practices were developed more than a thousand years ago. These ancient methods of joinery for building and furniture-making are complex and exquisite, yet incredibly functional without the need for glue or nails. The art of Japanese joinery has remained in practice through the centuries by highly trained craftsmen using intricate, hand-held tools. The purpose of this book is to introduce you to this fascinating craft and share some of the key skills you can develop to begin your training journey.

Throughout this book, you will learn about the theory, the specialties within this ancient profession, and the materials traditionally used. You will also learn about the different types of joins synonymous with Japanese carpentry and about the tools required to create them.

Within this book are four practical exercises that will lay the foundations for your journey into mastering Japanese joinery. You will begin by practicing a simple task and move forward into basic furniture items to hone your skills. Each exercise will prepare you for the next stage of your training.

To begin, it is vital to take some time to explore Japanese history and culture. These facts will help you understand this country's elegant belief system surrounding natural materials and building practices. Identifying with the country's history will also reveal how these unique techniques came to develop in such a different manner to western woodworking methods and what events led to these advancements in carpentry.

Japan is an island nation located in the northwest Pacific Ocean. The west coast of the country faces the Sea of Japan and extends from the Sea of Okhotsk in the north to the East China Sea and Taiwan in the south. Japan comprises an archipelago of 6,852 islands within the Pacific Ring of Fire. The five main islands from north to south are Hokkaido, Honshu, Shikoku, Kyushu, and Okinawa. The capital city of Tokyo is located on the central Pacific coast of Honshu.

Japan is a highly populated region with 126.2 million inhabitants. As a large proportion of the land is mountainous, the urbanized areas are mostly coastal, vastly populated, and narrow. Tokyo is the most populous metropolitan area in the world, with 34.7 of the country's people residing in the greater city area.

With around 73 percent of the land made up of dense forests and mountains, Japan has a stunning landscape, mostly untouched by human development. The majority of the land is unsuitable for habitation, industry, and so farming remains conserved for

nature and wildlife. A large network of national parks
has been established to protect the native wildlife of
the region.

Culturally, Japan is multifaceted and rich in
history and traditions, which has created a unique
development of civilization that sets the country apart
from the rest of the world in many ways.

During several centuries of a feudal era from 1185,
Japan was characterized by a ruling class of warriors,
named the Samurai, governing in concordance with
the Imperial Court. This was a military-dominated
government system defined in history by invasion
attempts from the Mongol armies, attempted
rebellions, and civil wars between feudal lords. Within
this era, prosperity was achieved in farming,
population growth, and commerce. The popularity of
Buddhism, introduced from China centuries before,
spread from the elite classes to the general populace,
encouraged via the embracing of this religion among
the samurai.

Within the feudal era trade, it was established with
Portuguese traders and Jesuit missionaries
introducing European technology and firearms to the
nation. The civil war and feuding were of great benefit
to the Portuguese who were able to trade firearms
with the Japanese armies. Small pockets of Christian
colonies emerged with some success in converting
Buddhist Japanese locals to the religion. Portuguese
became the first western language to receive a

Japanese dictionary as the Jesuits hoped this would aid more conversions to Catholicism.

Introducing European weaponry to the warring factions of Japan led to an imbalance of power with rivals seeking to conquer each other. The Japanese were also inspired to launch two failed invasion attempts of Korea. After an open war broke out between rival clans in 1600, the ruling Tokugawa shogunate began designing measures and codes of conduct to control the rival factions and create political unity. This included strict penalties for social unrest, often harsh executions, and outlawing the practice of Christian religions, foreign books, and other western practices. Thus began the Edo period.

In 1639, these measures for peace and unity led to a significant decision that would greatly impact the development of Japanese culture for the next 200 years. This was the year the Tokugawa dynasty decreed Japan an isolationist state. This meant closing the country to further foreign influence that could potentially cause dissent among its people. A single trading post on the island of Dejima was allowed to remain open to the Dutch, who were the only Europeans able to step foot on Japanese soil. The country continued to trade with China and Korea, but the Japanese people were forbidden from building ocean vessels or traveling abroad. Any Japanese person who did were not permitted to return.

The Edo period created an encapsulated society within Japan, shielded from any outside influence. Where many other cultures of the world at this time were within a phase of exploration, cultural influence, and growth, Japan was focused on maintaining and developing its own unique culture.

This isolated period in Japanese history did not diminish cultural growth; instead, the opposite occurred. Numeracy and literacy flourished in both urban and rural areas, as schools were often attached to local shrines. Art and entertainment advanced, and a vast commercial publishing industry thrived. With less fixation on feuding, the merchant classes, growing in wealth, gained interest in social pursuits such as theatre and music. The unique elements of Japanese culture stemmed from tradition and history, were focused on and developed without changes caused by outside influence.

The Edo period also affected architecture for public buildings and dwellings. During the Feudal era, the Shinto tradition of building around gardens was adapted to suit defense. For example, spaces designed for gardens were re-purposed for training practices in the preparation for battle. Untraditional stone and brickwork were incorporated to protect important locations from potential attacks. As unity grew and fighting diminished, the popularity of Buddhist and Shinto influenced buildings once again became popular. As the populace grew, dwellings with two stories were more common.

Traditional Japanese architecture was heavily influenced by nearby Asian countries, especially China. Although several styles and geographical differences created attributes unique to Japan. The buildings synonymous with the country are connected to the two main religions—Buddhist temples and tea houses, and Shinto shrines.

The most common and vital building material within Japanese architecture is wood. Japan has a vast amount of forests, and this has always been a key resource utilized for building. Wood is a deeply honored material in Japan as the Shinto belief system encompasses profound respect and worship of nature.

Shinto is a belief system that reveres nature. The religion's spiritual practices and rituals are based on the belief that the Kami (spiritual beings connected to elements of nature) are embodiments of the power of nature. Nature is worshipped, and a balance is sought between humanity and the mysterious power of nature to create a mutual harmony. Shrines have been traditionally built as sites of spiritual importance where this worship can take place. Collectively, these shrines are viewed as an interconnected web of entry points to the Kami, where human worship can be communicated.

The reverence of nature inspires an elegant relationship with wood as a building material for the Japanese that is unique to this culture. The forest is sacred, so wood is treated with huge respect by carpenters and craftsmen. Within Japanese joinery, there is terminology for joins made, using different elements of the tree. Yukiatsugi is the joining of two ends taken from the top of the tree's trunk. Wakaretsugu is the joining of two ends taken from the base of the tree's trunk. Okuritsugu is the joining of a piece from each of these parts of the tree.

Japanese architecture has also been greatly shaped by geographical disasters. The Japanese archipelago is positioned within the Pacific ring of fire, a horseshoe-shaped area located within the Pacific Ocean where several tectonic plates meet. The ring of fire is the most active earthquake belt on Earth, making the area also prone to underwater volcanoes and subsequent tsunamis.

Destructive earthquakes, often resulting in tsunamis, tend to occur in Japan several times each century. Whereas in low earthquake risk areas of the world, humans naturally developed building practices using earth and stone, the Japanese found that wooden structures built with the use of complex joins had a better chance of surviving the frequent disasters of their region.

Japanese joinery has been developed to withstand and counteract the level of damage from earthquakes, but also to create incredibly strong building frameworks capable of bearing huge weight. Wood is carefully selected and often aged within these practices. Woods are also selected for the beauty and quality of the grain, as nature is respected and is a very present symbol of Japanese cultural themes. The Cypress Hanoi has been the most sought and used wood for more than 1,000 years.

Traditional Japanese buildings feature a structure of posts and lintels supporting a gently curved roof. The inner walls are never load-bearing, often paper-thin, and generally movable. The internal layout with adjustable screen walls allows for the space to adapt as required for the purpose. These types of walls, named shoji, also mean less destruction from earthquakes and are more easily replaceable. The roofs of these structures are wider than the internal space from all sides. This requires a complex bracket system of beams known as Tokyo. This bracket system is more elaborate in shrines and larger buildings, and more simplified in domestic buildings.

The relationship between the inside and outside is somewhat interchangeable for public buildings and homes as the garden and nature are seen as important, according to Shinto beliefs. The interchangeable moving walls incorporate this relationship for ease of access and views into the garden or surrounding natural environment. For temples, this feature opens the building for the presence of visitors.

Unlike western buildings where the structural components are usually hidden beneath plaster or paneling, the structural elements of Japanese buildings are displayed. These wooden frames, beams, and posts are a sublime blend of form and function that add to the overall beauty and ornamentation of the building.

Both internally and externally, Japanese buildings aesthetics adhere to a minimal and simple but elegant style. These visual ideals stem from Shinto and Chinese Taoism. Natural materials are present, not only in the wooden structural elements, but also in the rice straw mats, paper and silk wall treatments, and bamboo screen frames. This idea of minimal and natural beauty is still present today in contemporary Japanese architecture and interior design.

Japanese joinery techniques have also been influential throughout the country's history for furniture design. The themes of elegance, functionality, simplicity, and minimalism are also transferred onto the interior spaces. Negative space is viewed as being important as the necessity for functional lifestyle items, so every item is deliberate and exact. As furniture is traditionally crafted from wood, the intricate joinery for strength and function are as vital as for structures. The interchangeable nature of interior spaces adds an essential function to furniture—the ability to be easily moved between spaces. This lifestyle factor has created several design features to be common within the design of these items, such as handles for lifting, minimal decorative effects, and lightness for movement.

Chapter One:
What Is Japanese Joinery?

Japanese carpentry is renowned globally for its highly refined craft and precision. The delicate balance between complex technique and elegant simplicity can best be described as 'geometry meets nature'. In this chapter, Japanese joinery will be explored in detail, delving further into the history, the techniques, and some examples of traditional Japanese structures synonymous with this building style.

Having an interest in woodworking connects a person to a long history of craftsmanship spanning human civilization. Many people begin this journey during their school years, learning the basic skills required to complete simple tasks, become comfortable with physical tools, and invoke interest in this activity. This study may lead to a lifelong enthusiasm for carpentry as a hobby, or potentially a profession.

Wood is a natural material, and its response to different tools and crafting methods can be understood from considering the tree. Trees grow upward and outward with each season marked with rings that are visible within the grain as sections are cut. The growing pattern of the tree needs to be considered in terms of directionality for cutting to get the best performance from the wood. The Japanese profoundly respect the tree, as well as the wood. To follow Shinto practices, the tree informs building decisions. For example, wood taken from the south-facing part of the tree's trunk will be reverentially used in the creation of the south-facing side of the building or shrine.

Understanding the relationship between wood and the craftsman is of huge value to anyone working with this material, like any other physical material. Cultivating this relationship through practice and experimentation will inform dexterity, ability, and accomplishment. No piece of wood is the same; the grain is as unique as a human fingerprint. The Japanese select each piece of wood thoughtfully and deliberately, and this is a beneficial lesson to apply to any kind of woodworking practice.

Many people incorrectly believe that woodworking can be hard labor and difficult when using hand tools. However, when tools are properly sharpened and cared for, the tools will do much of the hard work without a lot of force at all. Sharpening chisels, saws, and planes are especially important for Japanese joinery where precision is vital, and too much force could result in destroying a day's work on a complex range of shapes.

Before attempting Japanese joinery, it is advisable to already be familiar with the tools and methods used for cutting and shaping wooden objects. Coarse tools are best for coarse work, and fine tools are best for fine work.

It is also important to have a suitable space and basic workshop equipment available. This need not be any more than a simple workbench in a garage or shed. Having a designated space will help to create a suitable headspace for concentrating on the tasks to be achieved. When focusing on fine work, as is needed for joinery, comfort and free movement are key. Therefore, it is useful to test where the best place to stand will be, whether a stool is required, and where wooden pieces can be clamped in place for precise cutting. It is a Japanese custom to sit on rice straw mats on the floor, but this may not be comfortable for everyone.

In modern architecture, materials are factory cut and fabricated to exert as much control as possible to achieve precision and replication. Ancient Japanese craftsmen, the Shokunin, did not need such machines to achieve the same precisely repeated shapes and elements. Many of the world's oldest surviving wooden structures can be found in Japan, created with joinery techniques.

The shokunin did not select wood for uniformity; instead, they selected it by using the unique attributes of the tree as an advantage. Inconsistencies were masterfully balanced and counteracted, and the entire life of the wood was utilized. Shokunin are able to understand and anticipate the behavior of the wood over time—how it would expand and contract depending on climate variation, how it would inevitably shrink with age, and which position would suit it best due to its previous living state as the tree.

These skills were often the difference between a building surviving an earthquake or being destroyed. The results show a sophisticated technological mastery that is astounding for the period of history in which they originated. These methods of manufacture are far more robust than many modern ones in use today. Modern manufacture also does not prepare for the same level of longevity, ease of replacing any damaged components, and potential for disassembly with minimal waste or environmental corruption.

The fundamental aspect of Japanese joinery is that only one material is used or required. The shokunin understood that wood has both the strength and flexibility to complement how it is joined, and the join will be long-lasting. In Japanese joinery, the strength of the wood is used to both add and counteract its own weight and pressure in an elegant balance that is stronger than any nails or adhesive could be.

This is done by cutting complex geometric shapes into the ends of the wooden pieces that must be joined. These shapes are countered and symmetrical with each other, the negative space of one mirroring the physical space of the other precisely. The pieces are designed to neatly slot together, sometimes using an additional pin-shaped piece slotting from an alternate angle. The direction of joining is the opposite of the pressure of weight that will be placed on the join, meaning that once interlocked, the two pieces are immovable.

These methods adhere to the Buddhist and Shinto principles of respecting nature. As the tree must be cut down to build the structure, the carpenter owes a debt for the life of the tree. By using the wood to create something both long-lasting and beautiful to behold, that debt is settled. It is intended that the structure will exist for as long as the tree may have lived untampered with. By fulfilling this ideal, the spirits connected with trees will be appeased.

An important example that demonstrates the astounding skill of the shokunin, and the spiritual principles applied to the building, is the famous Horyu-Ji Temple. This temple, located in the ancient capital of Nara, is the oldest wooden structure in the world. The temple was originally built in 600AD, then re-built in 700AD after a lightning strike caused a devastating fire. For context, this was the time frame in which the Mayan empire was prospering, the Anglo Saxons were reclaiming the British Isles from the Roman Empire, and the Chinese were discovering the formula for gunpowder. At this point, the Japanese were designing and building structures with wood that would last more than a thousand years and still be going strong today.

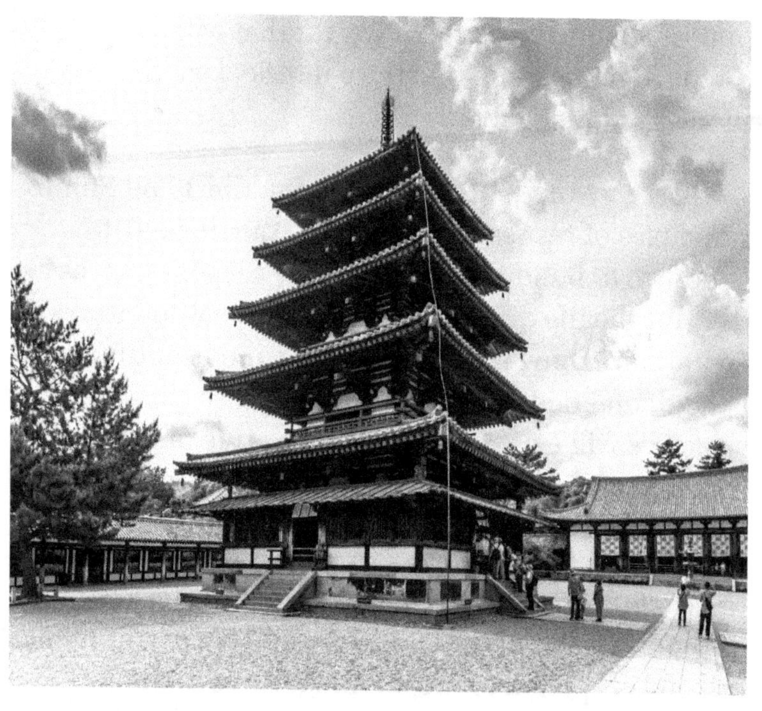

The Horyu-Ji, a temple in Irakuga, Nara Prefecture, Japan. Image by RPBaiao

The Pagoda is the oldest building within the temple complex and now also serves as a Buddhist museum, housing many of the religion's most priceless Japanese objects and educating visitors on the story of Buddhism in Japan.

It was built using 2000-year-old Japanese cypress (hinoki). The trees were cut and prepared using handheld tools, nothing like the saws and machinery used today in harvesting lumber. The carpenters also carefully selected the wood, understanding how each part would behave due to the tree's position, angle toward the sun, and quality of the soil where it was located. All of these factors were considered and taken into account for the wood's likelihood to expand or bend with moisture, which direction a bend may occur, and any potential for rot. Each piece of wood was then designated a suitable placement within this complex structure that would make the most from its unique characteristics and would demonstrate respect for the tree that was sacrificed.

The temple complex is reflective of a traditional Chinese Buddhist monastery plan. It is laid out on a north-to-south axis, with a south-facing entrance. In addition to the Pagoda, the complex includes the main hall, lecture hall, north gate, and the Great South Gate. The complex is surrounded by a walled corridor with a colonnaded interior and walled exterior. This cloistered walkway has several Chinese features, such as wood columns, window openings, and plaster exterior walls.

The complex differs slightly from traditional Chinese design in that the Pagoda and Kondo (lecture hall) are offset, instead of symmetrical placement. This is believed to be for a visual purpose so that all of the structures can be viewed simultaneously from various angles when approached by visitors.

Temples and shrines in Japan used to be the tallest structures in the country. The Horyu-Ji Pagoda is five stories tall and stands at 122 feet in total. The structure is partially supported by one central column rising the entire height. Outer columns with cantilever brackets support the five roofs. Each roof surrounds the structure, curving upward and inward, and these roofs diminish in size with each floor to enhance the height of the structure. To support these roofs and their heavy tiles, complex framing brackets with interlocking joins were constructed. Joinery techniques were also utilized for the staircases, floor platforms, inner walls, railings, banisters, window frames, and the plethora of ornamental wooden details within the building's interior and exterior.

The design of the landmark curved roofs of the temple and other traditional buildings is a definitive Buddhist style. The curvature of this roof shape is a complex structure to realize without mathematical input. The slope and turned up eaves require a geometrical system for ensuring repetition and symmetry. Without knowledge of the mathematical equations required for exact repetition (which were not introduced until the 18th century), carpenters worked by eye and with practical measurement methods. Line drafting and a standard carpenter's square were used to drawing the angles and lines for cutting on the surface of the wood.

The posts' and beams' structural style used for Buddhist temples and other traditional Japanese buildings is known as a 'rigid frame' structure. The type of joinery predominantly used for securing the posts and beams are mortise and tenon connections, with the use of wooden pegs and wedges that slot into the two pieces. This method, whilst very strong, provides a level of flexibility within the structure that allows for expansion and contraction of the wood due to climate and also for preventing damage from earthquakes.

This famous landmark gives an idea of the incredible skill that Japanese carpentry requires, and its uses in practice for the joinery that this book describes.

In a nutshell, Japanese joinery is all about how to make joints with hand tools such as a chisel, hammer, mallet, saw, and others without using any fastener like screws, nails, and even glue.

Chapter Summary

In the next chapter, the techniques of Japanese joinery will be explored further, illuminating the different styles, how they are created, and for what they are typically used. However, this chapter dealt with the meaning of Japanese joinery from the pre-history time to present-day Japan and how it has affected wood construction in its entirety.

Chapter Two:
Japanese Joinery and Techniques

In this section of this chapter, the different styles of Japanese joinery will be explored in greater detail and explained with examples of what type of structure the join is traditionally used to build. A suitable way to envision and describe the intricate joints of Japanese joinery is by considering it as a three-dimensional puzzle that is simple from the outside, yet complex from within. Once the mechanism is understood, the puzzle is easy to solve.

The joints described in this section can be created with a range of complexity. For a beginner, the joints can be constructed in a manageable and uncomplicated manner. Once the basic skills and understanding have been mastered, more complicated joints can be explored.

Before investigating these joins, it will be helpful to become familiar with the terminology used to describe them. The guide below is a helpful reference to learn and follow these words within the descriptions:

- **Tenon**: This is a protruding piece of wood designed to fit into a slot (mortise).

- **Miter**: This is a cut made at 90 degrees into the main surface intended for a join bisecting this angle to form a corner.

- **Rails**: This describes horizontal lengths of wood in frame and panel construction.

- **Stiles**: This describes vertical lengths of wood in frame and panel construction.

- **Spline**: This is a strip of wood that is inserted into grooves cut in the edges of the interior corner of a frame.

- **Dado**: This is a slot cut into the surface of the wood to hold and counterbalance a shelf.

- **Mortise**: This is a hole or recess cut into the wood intended for a corresponding part (tenon) to slot into.

- **Bevel**: This is a tool used to layout and transfer angled lines for a miter cut.

A simple and effective method of making joints without using nails or screws

Here, we consider the mortise and tenon joint, which seems to be the oldest ways of joining two pieces of wood. It consists of a mortise hole and tenon tongue that fit into one another. As one of the versatile joints, mortise and tenon can be applied in many different woodworking types including fine furniture, framed buildings, and many others.

To make this particular joint, the following tools are required, including tenon saw, mortise chisel, steel rule, mortise gauge, marking knife, steel square, pencil, and clamp. Just follow these steps.

Step one: Prepare materials for the two parts of the joint.

Step two: Mark the sizes on the wood. Use 'Rule of Thirds' to set out the sizes. What this rule implies is that the proportions of the joint will be divided into three parts. So, if the tenon rail measures 20mm in thickness, the mortise chisel should be almost one-third of it, which is approximately 7mm.

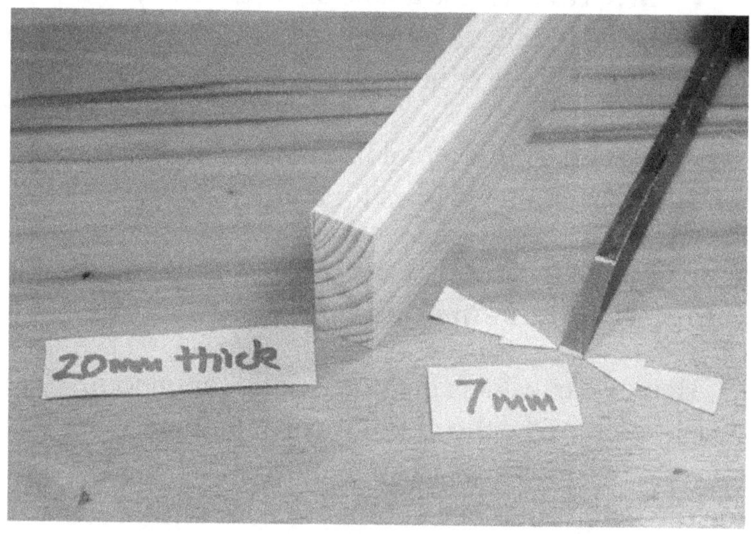

Step three: Adjust the mortise gauge pins to the width of the chisel.

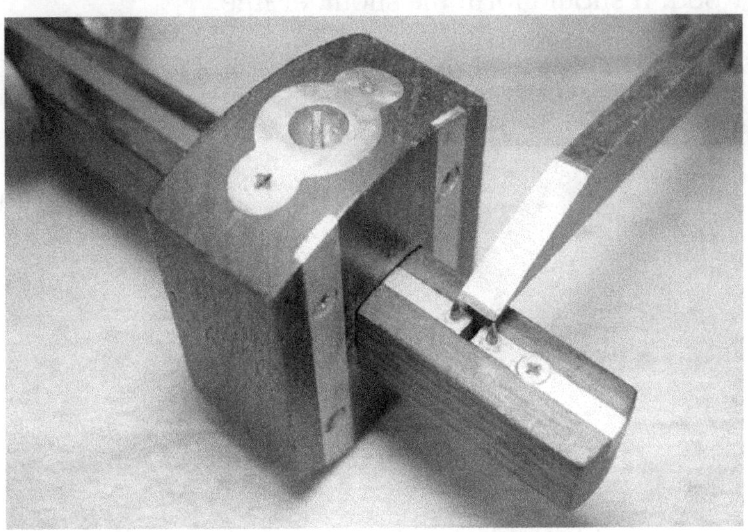

Step four: Make two arrowed dots and examine each side to ensure the tenon is centrally placed.

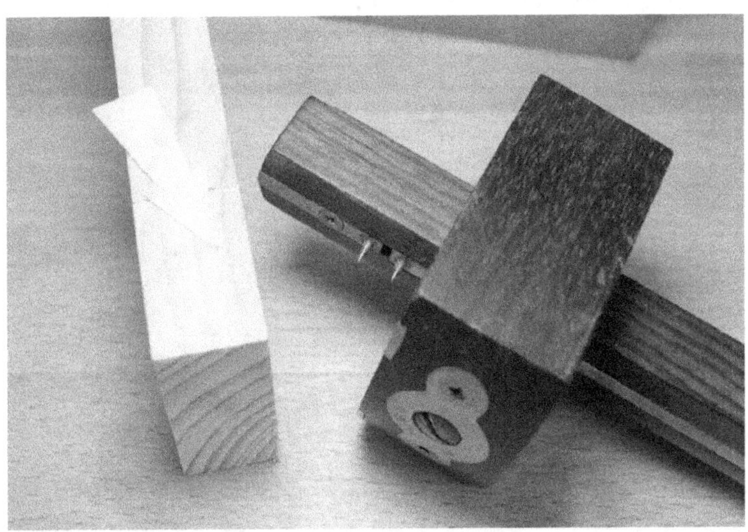

Step five: Mark the depth of the tenon to be almost two-thirds of the depth of the second piece of wood. It should form the shoulder line.

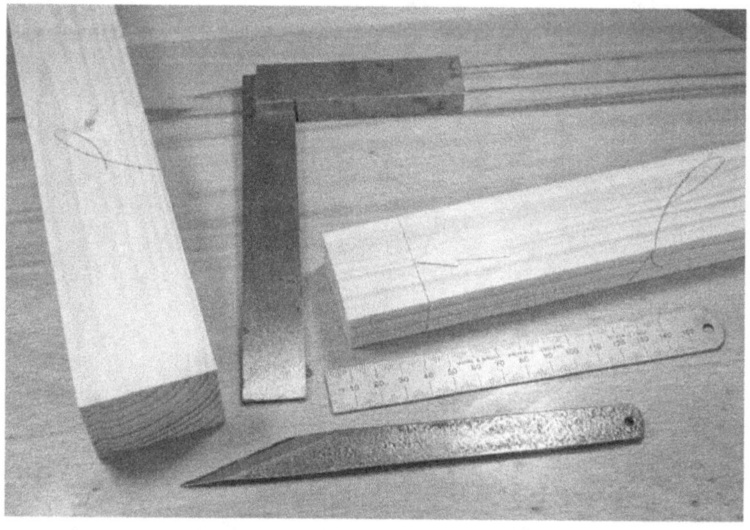

Step six: Mark parallel lines all around while holding the wood in the vice.

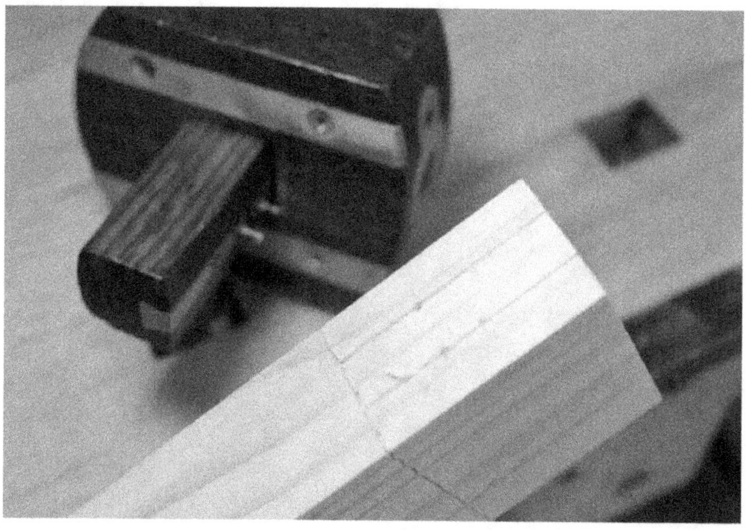

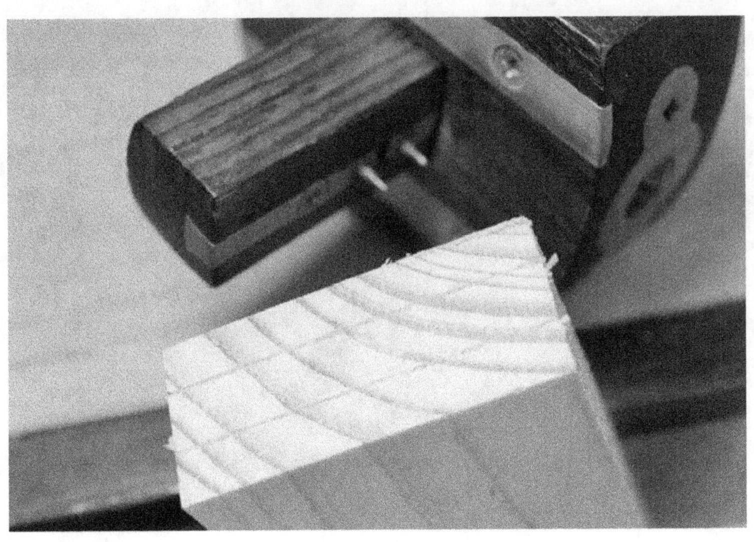

Step seven: Set marking gauge to 6mm and measure line all the way around.

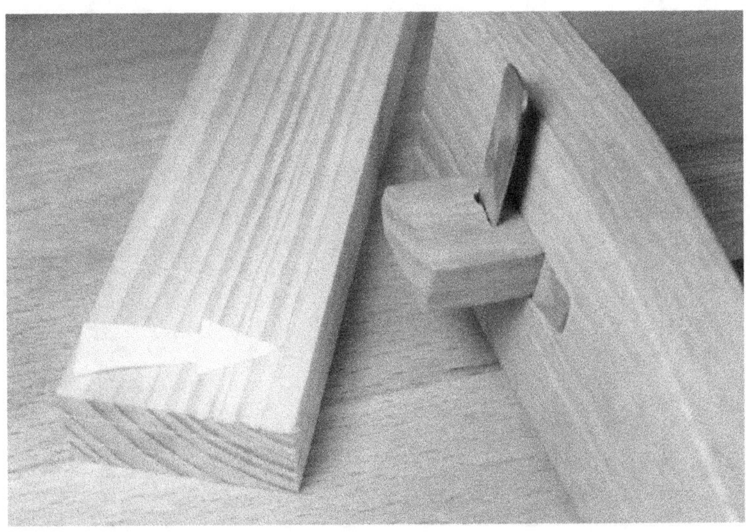

Step eight: Set a marking gauge to the wood's width, which is 6mm, and mark the width of the tenon.

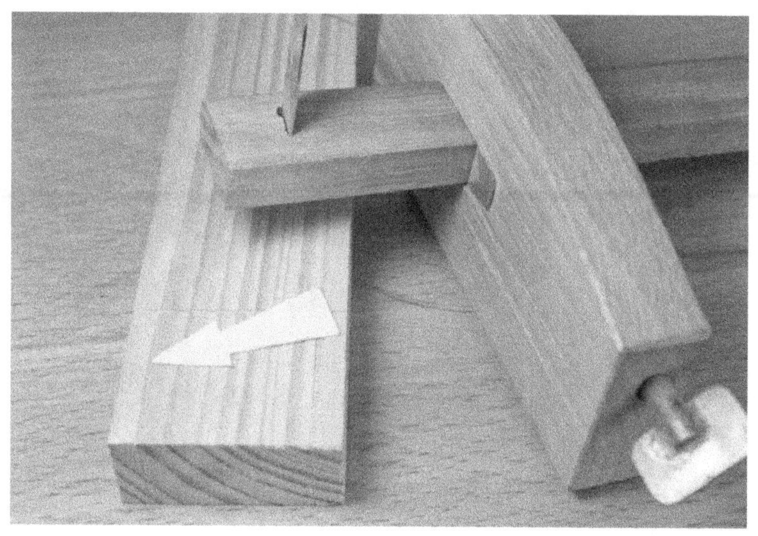

Here comes the completed marking out of tenon end grain.

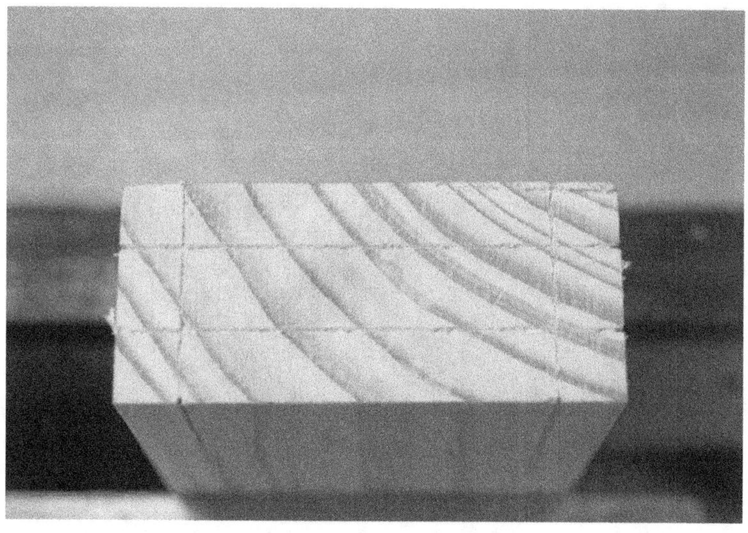

Step 10: Lay tenon wood piece on mortise material and mark the position of mortise using a pencil. Then, transfer lines to the wood.

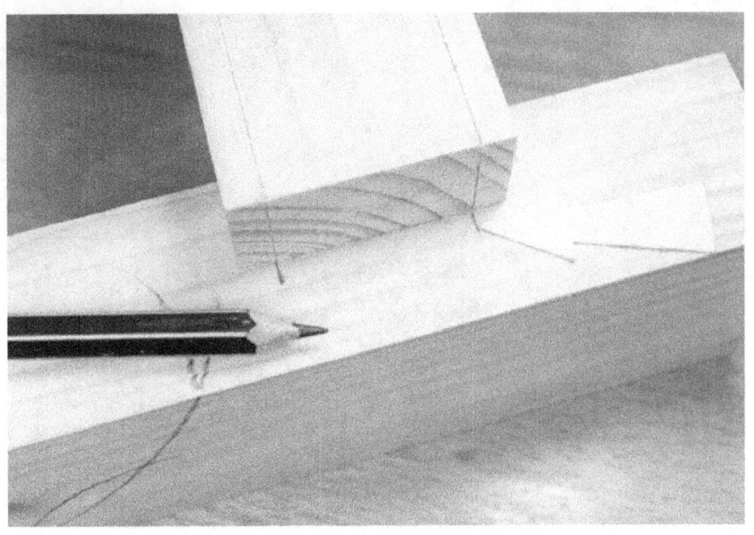

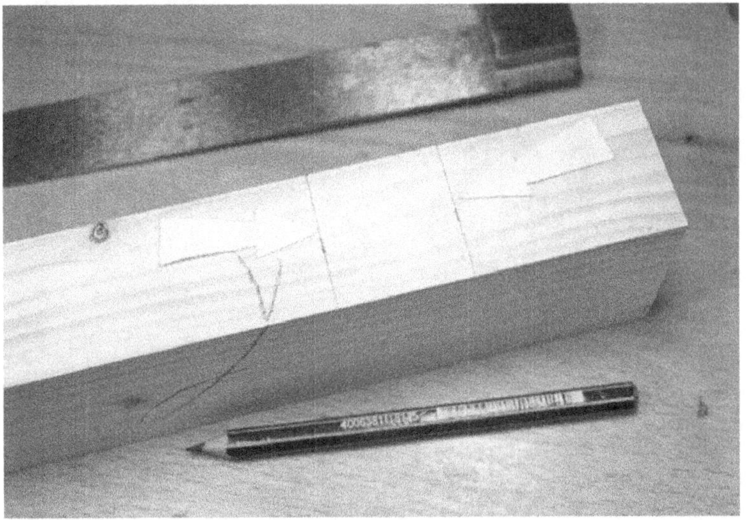

Step 11: Set mortise gauge to mark the position of the mortise, and do not change the distance between the pins. You can mark the width of the mortise with the knife.

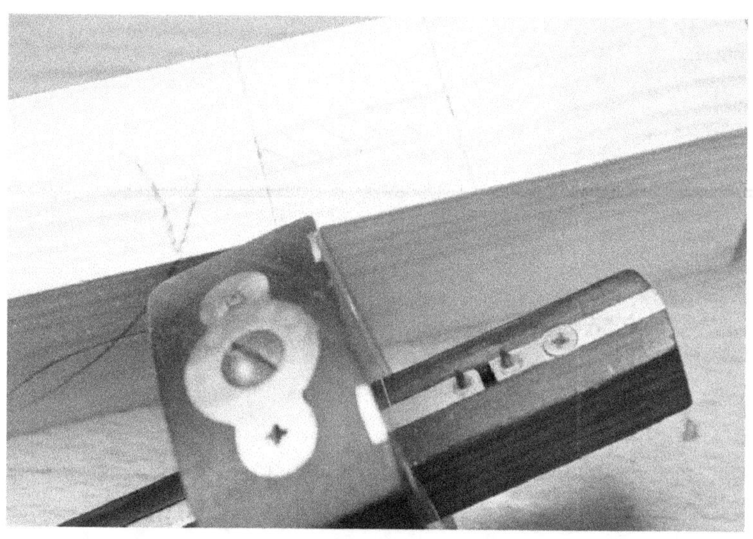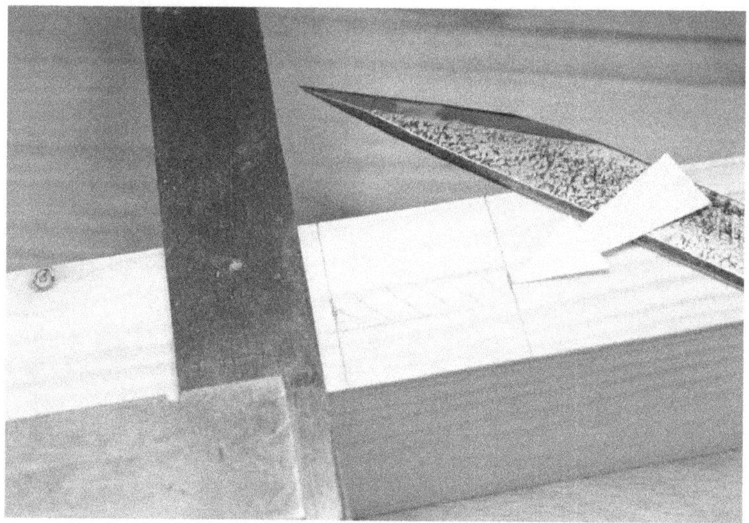

Step 12: Clamp the mortise position over the bench and chop off the mortise. Stand at the end of the bench and align the chisel vertically when chopping the mortise.

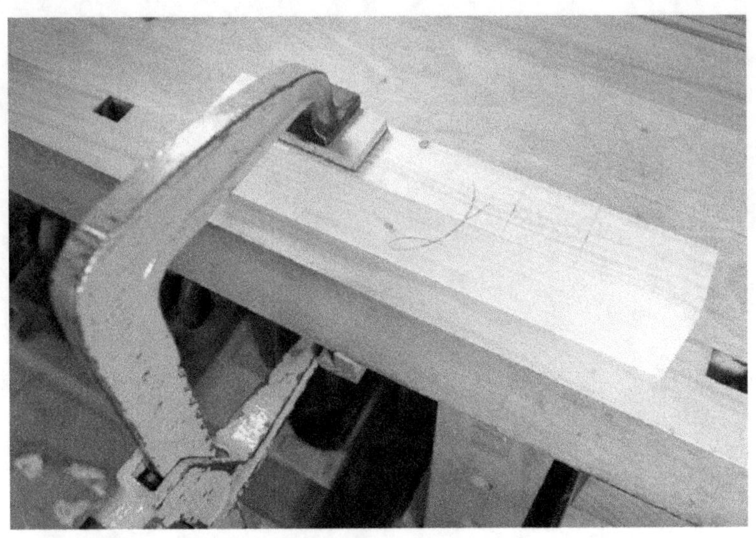

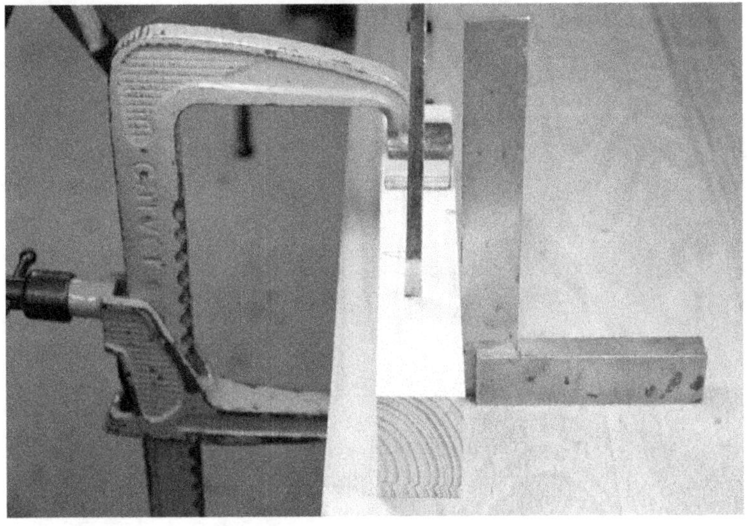

Step 13: Chop off the waste with the chisel as a lever to remove the chippings. Stop at 2mm from the knife line.

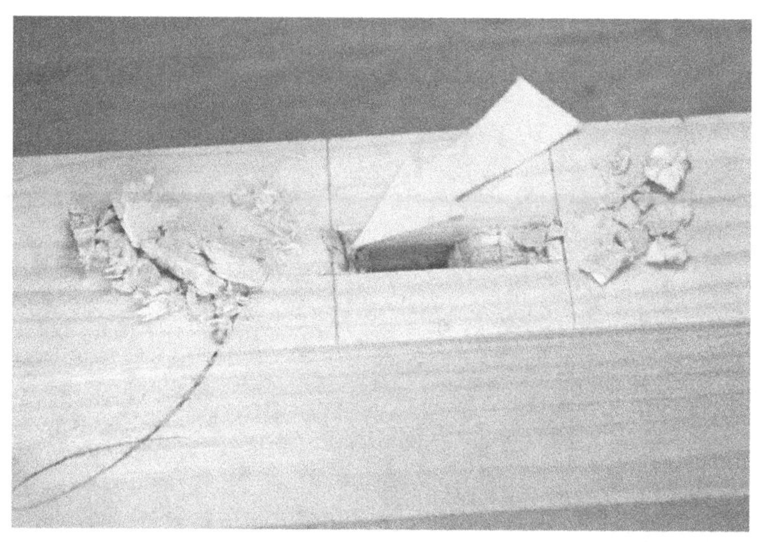

Step 14: Check to see if the depth is 3mm longer than the tenon.

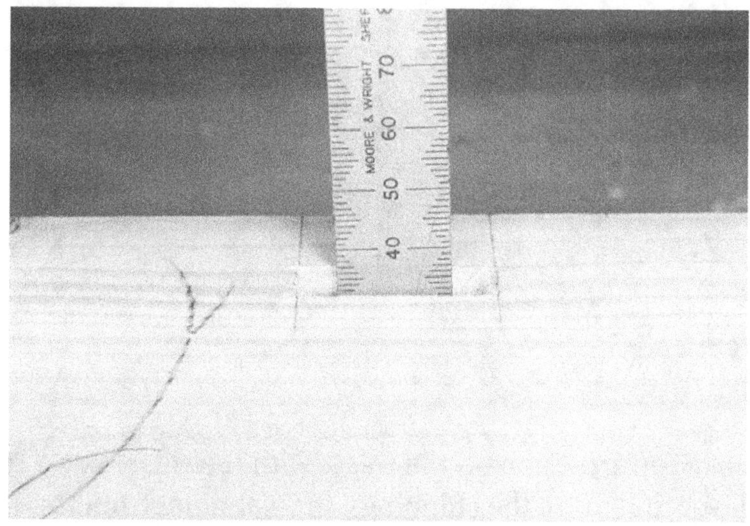

Step 15: Make two final cuts, one at each end on the knife line. Check it with the square.

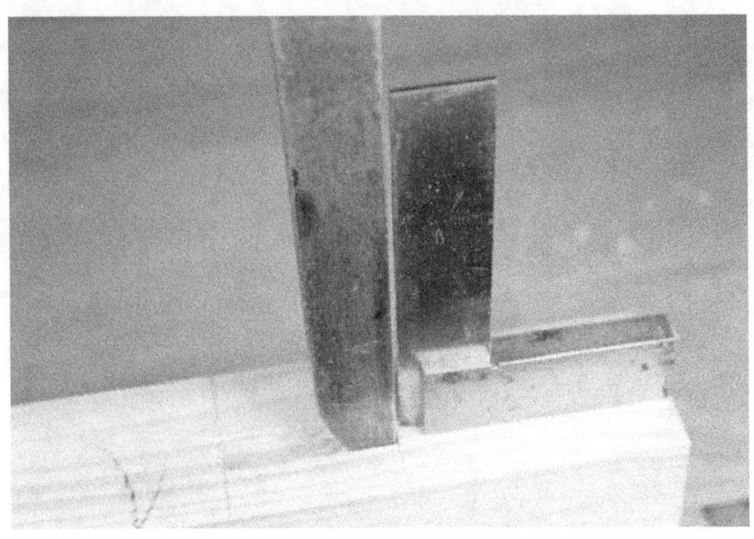

Step 16: Cut the tenon by hand using a hand saw to make two triangular cuts, one for each side.

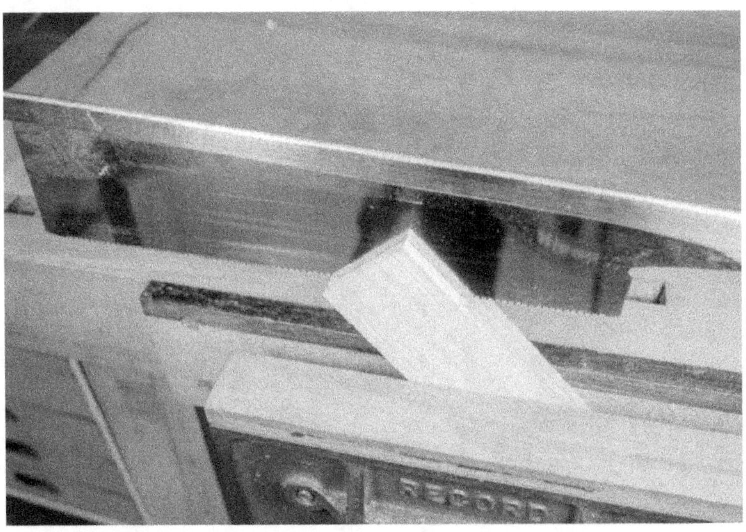

Step 17: Finish the cutting by sawing in the horizontal direction to the shoulder line.

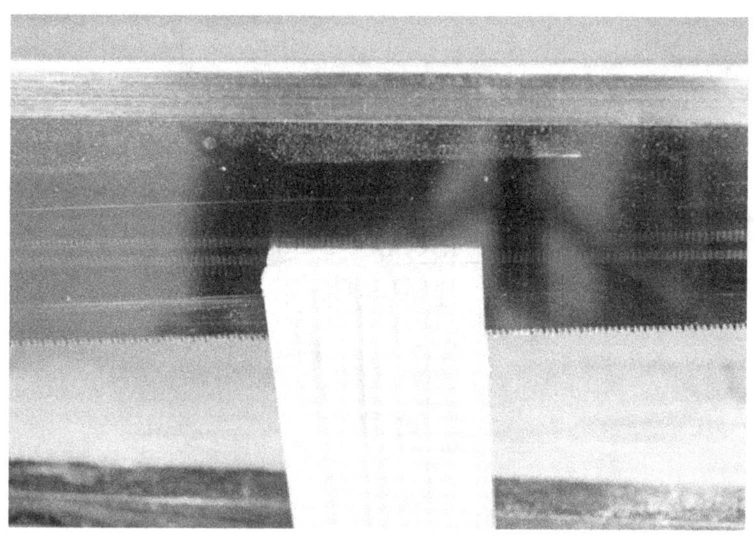

Step 18: Make two additional cuts on the face of the board.

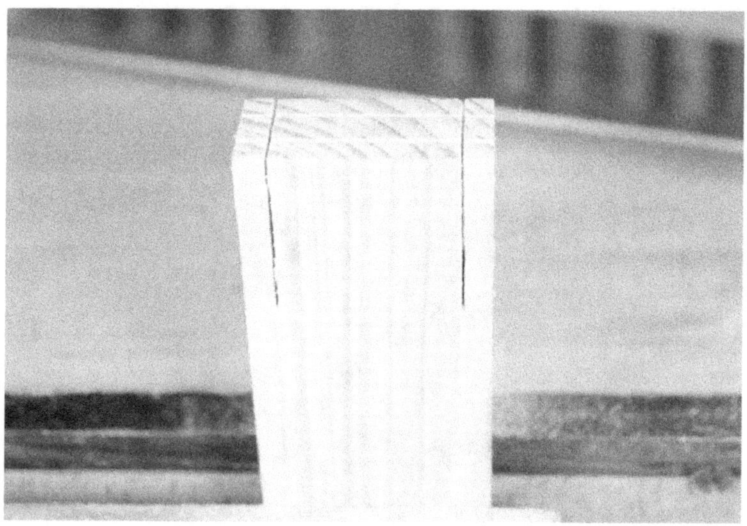

Step 19: Position tenon piece on the bench hook and saw off cheeks from tenon all round, leaving 0.5mm waste from the shoulder line.

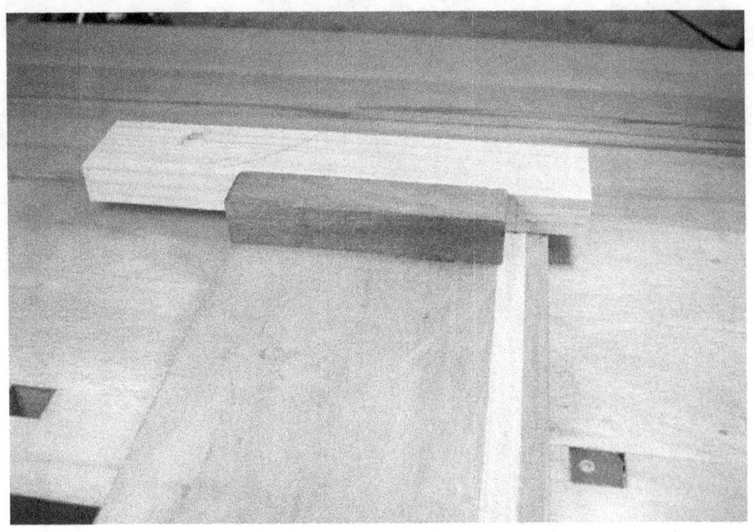

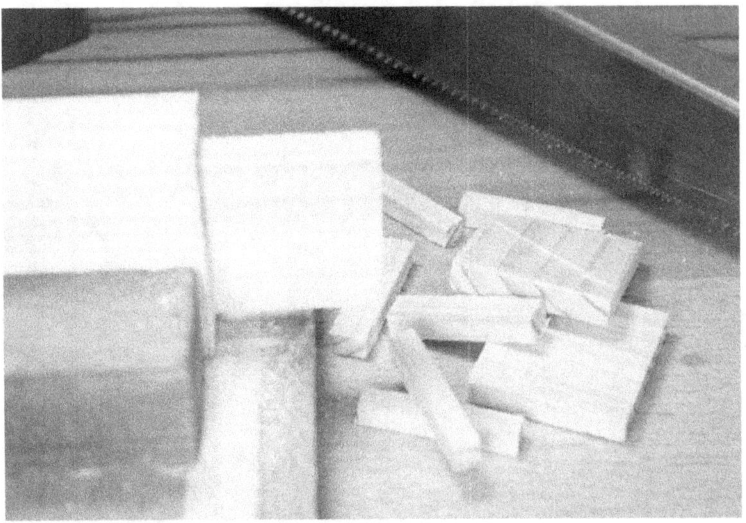

Step 20: Place the wide chisel on the knife line, look for the square, and chop off the shoulder line. Then, use the block plane to chamfer the end of the tenon.

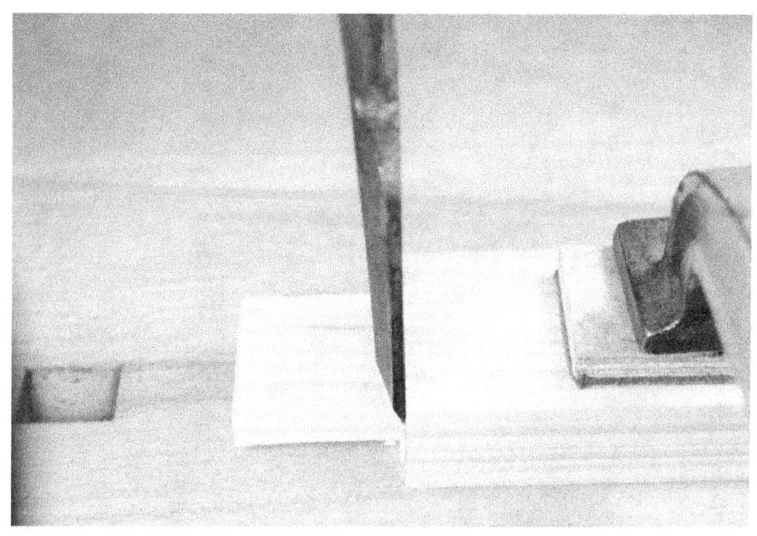

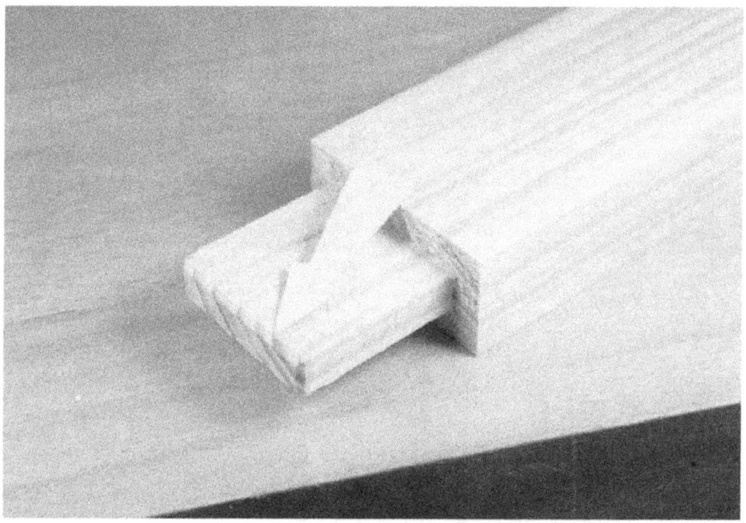

Remember, the joint should push together with moderate hand pressure applied as seen in the picture below.

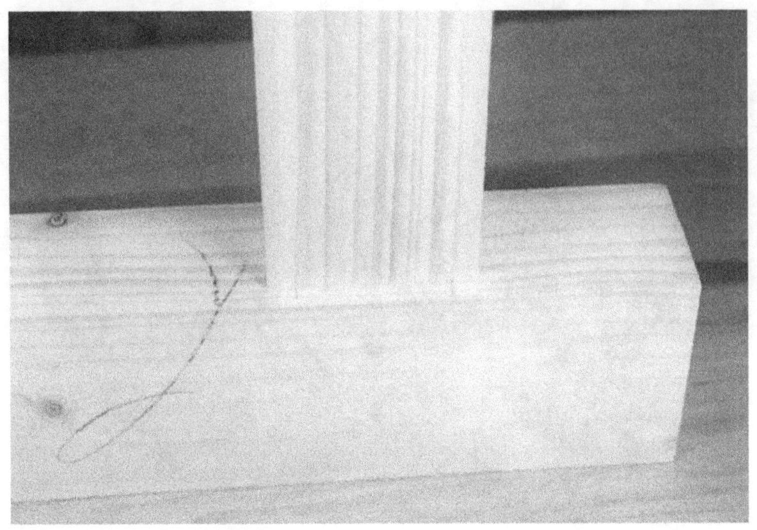

Special characteristics of various joints and their specialized use

Presented below are the various joints with their unique characteristics, as well as specialized uses.

Interlocking Tenon Joint

The interlocking tenon joint is generally used for the creation of staircases and making chairs. Three pieces of wood can be joined together in a cross shape, such as the seat platform joined to each leg of a chair. The leg features a cross-type cut, leaving space for two rails to the slot and lock together placed from above. The rails feature a central square-shaped cut designed to affix the two pieces within the interior of the cross-shaped cut-out of the leg.

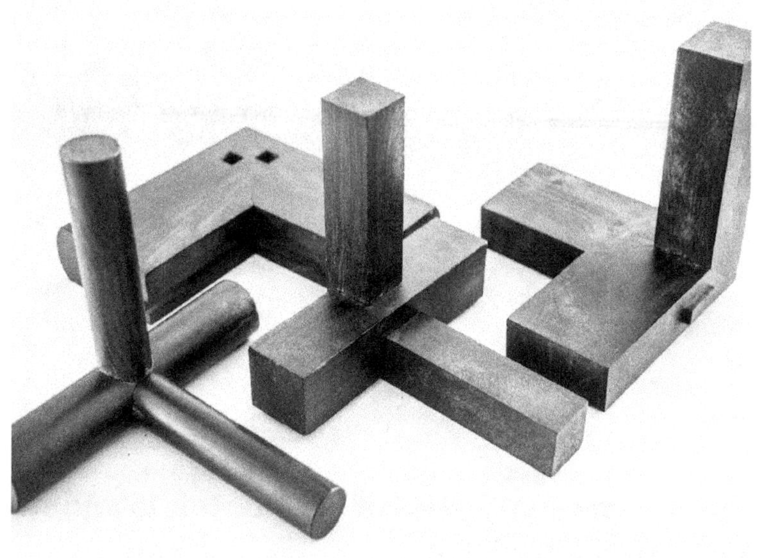

Interlocking Miter Joint

The interlocking miter joint is popular in heavy frame construction. Two pieces of wood are joined to create a right angle. Each end of each piece is chiseled to form a half-lap with mitered shoulders protruding at a 45-degree angle. The two tenons are shaped similarly to arrowheads that overlap each other inside the mortise with a step-type shape. The two pieces slot together leaving a slot open for a thin spline that secures the join in place and prevents movement.

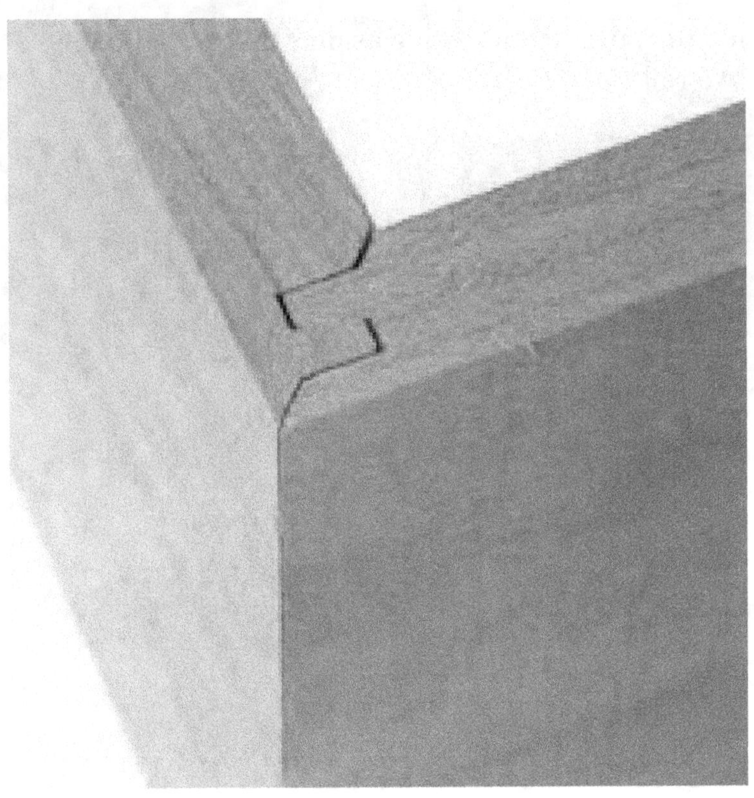

Three-way Corner Miter Joint

The three-way corner miter joint is often used for tables, such as desks and dining tables. All three pieces feature miters, and the table leg has a tenon that fits into notches cut into the other two pieces (rails). The leg's end forms a pointed triangular shape on the outer side fitting into a corresponding shaped mortise on each rail. On the inside, a square-shaped tenon cleanly covers the join within. For thicker rails that require a sturdier reinforced joint, a three-way pinned corner joint is very similar, but the leg section features two tenons acting as pins that slot into the two rails.

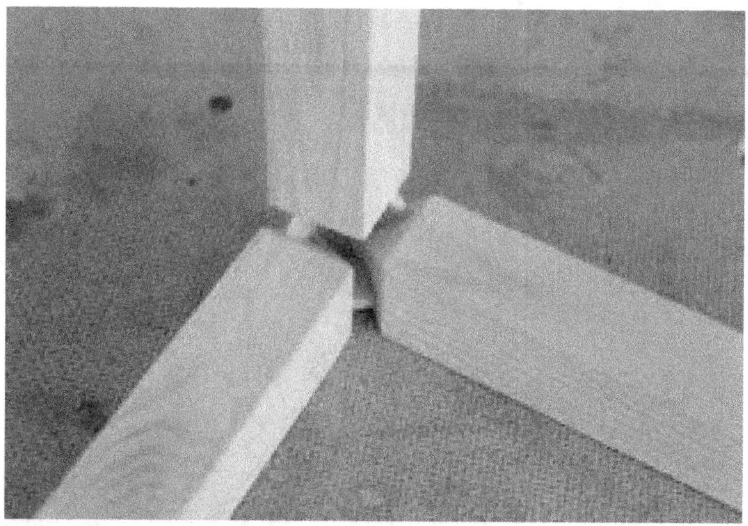

Full Blind Dovetail Joint

The full blind dovetail joint is also sometimes known as the secret mitered dovetail joint. These types of joints are used in furniture-making to join the sides of a cabinet or box. Of all types of dovetail joints, these are considered the strongest. Alternating angled grooves, similar to teeth, are chiseled from the interior sides of each piece of wood to be joined. A lip is left on the exterior walls of the wooden panels that will meet as the dovetails join, disguising the complex teeth. The two sides then neatly slot together in a joint that is invisible from the outside.

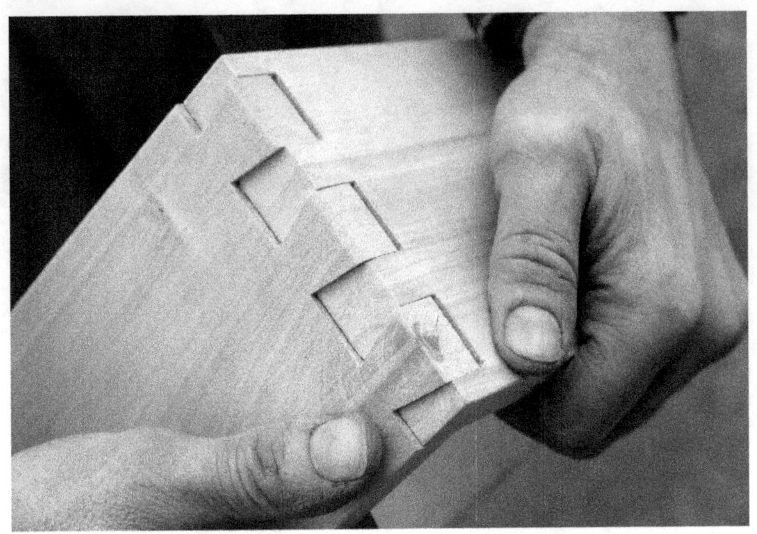

Sliding Dovetail Joint

The sliding dovetail joint is often used to join rails to legs in chair construction. This joining technique features tenon and miter shapes that slide together with a stabilizing tenon to reinforce the join. The legs and rails come together forming 90-degree angles, suitable for a seating platform.

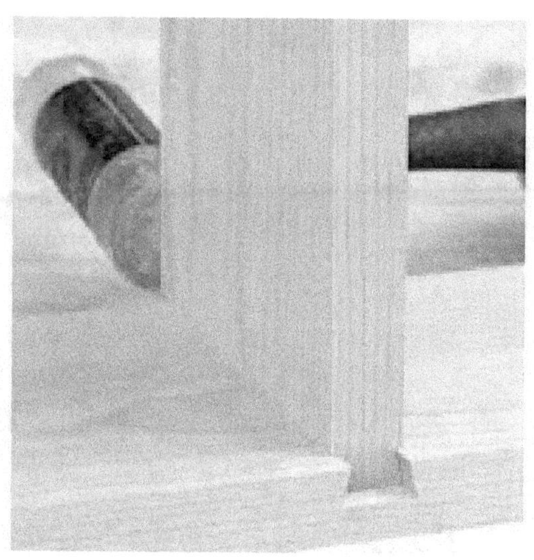

Shelf Support Joint

The shelf support joints are designed and used for shelves that can bear heavy loads. A dado is required to be cut into a vertical wooden section to support the horizontal shelf. The dado has blind tenon cut-outs corresponding to the shapes cut into the horizontal shelf to match the stopped dado. The tenons can be of varying shapes and sizes, depending on what is best for the shelf length and type of panel it will be joined to. The join must be tight to support the weight of the shelf and load.

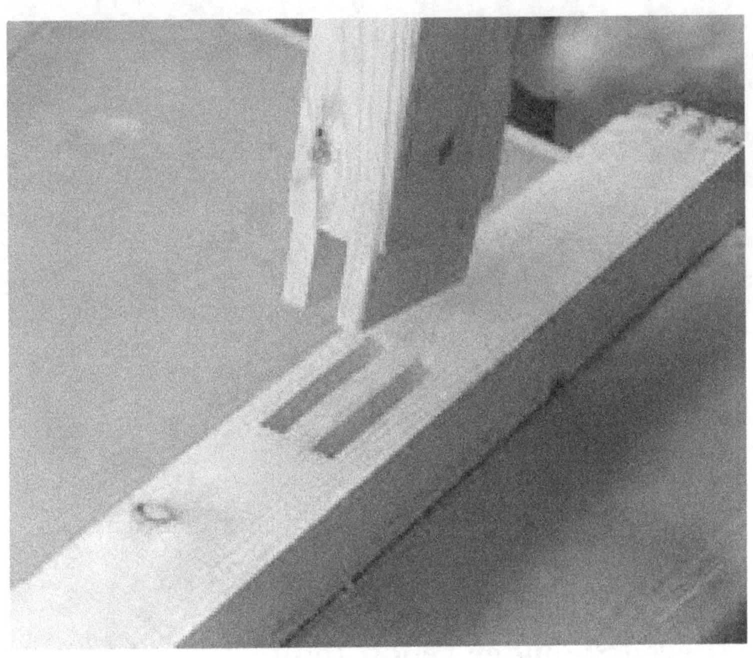

Divided Mortise and Tenon Joint

The divided mortise and tenon joint is used for large frame and panel pieces used in the construction of doors and other features within buildings and furniture, such as cabinets. Tenons are cut into the rails to fit through the stile's mortise. The rails often join together through the stile, combining three pieces in a cross-type shape. When this is the case, the tenon and mortise join the two rails in the slot together within the opening of the stile, neatly hiding the join.

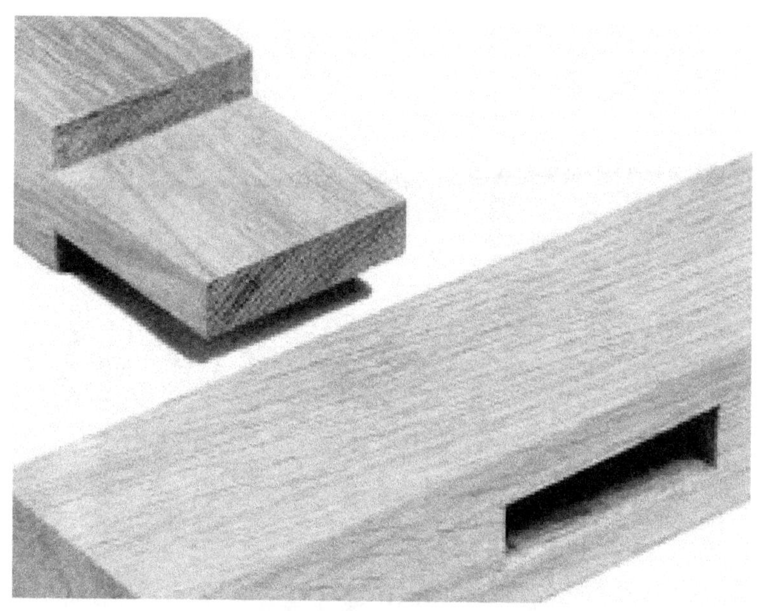

Mitered Shoulder Tenon Joint

The mitered shoulder tenon joint has a similar purpose as the divided mortise and tenon joints for the construction of frame and panel structures and objects. The difference is that the surfaces bordering the mortise and tenons on one side are beveled, creating angled joining shapes. This creates a pleasing "X" shape where the three wooden pieces meet, which enhances the unique attributes of each piece of wood and their grain patterns.

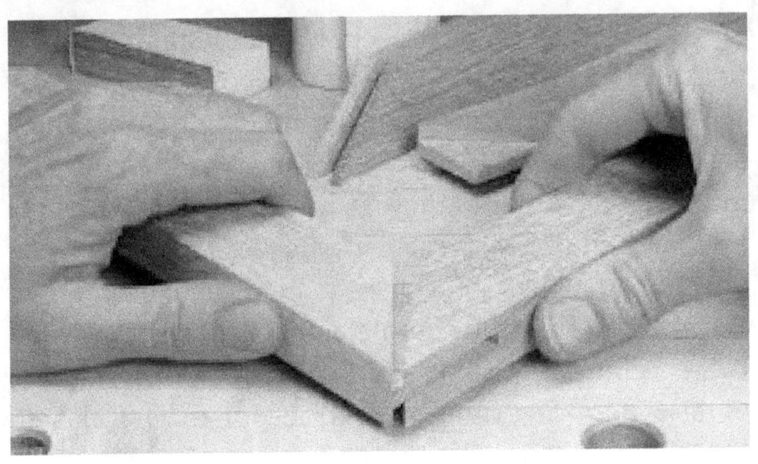

Mitered Corner Joint

The mitered corner joint joins two pieces of wood together to create a 90-degree angle. The join itself forms a 45-degree angle within the corner's interior. A concealed dovetail tenon in a triangular shape is cut from one edge to slot into a matching mortise on the other edge. The two pieces are combined with no visible evidence of the internal join. This type of join is typically used to create a large frame, such as a sliding door frame, or window frame. This join can be created with one tenon, or more than one by repeating the same shape, or asymmetrically cutting the triangular shapes and their corresponding mortises into the two wooden pieces.

The above Japanese joins are the basic methods used in ancient Japan, as well as today by carpenters all over the world. Using these joining designs, any manner of woodworking projects can be undertaken, from furniture to the structures of buildings.

Although it may have seemed unfathomable that the shokunin were able to achieve incredible large scale projects such as the Horyu-ji Temple complex using simple hand-made tools, breaking down the individual techniques they used aids in understanding. Every carpentry project is simply a series of small tasks performed one by one until the vision is realized and complete. Later in this book, these techniques will be put into practice via a series of tasks following small steps to accomplish a finished object.

Three joints that don't need any specialized tools, and how to make them

Here are three main joints that you can use to make virtually everything from cool shelves to rocking chairs.

Sliding Dovetail: The sliding dovetail is used for braces on doors. It is equally used to attach chair legs to a chair or stool seats, as well as chair legs to chair feet.

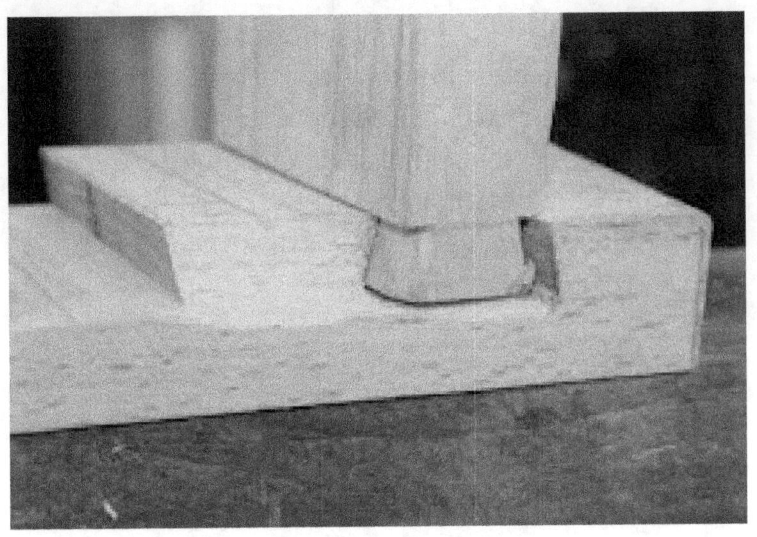

How to make a sliding dovetail

The first step is to lay out the dovetail so that it becomes narrow in both directions. The suitable edge angles range from 3 to 5 degrees.

Secondly, cut the dovetail out, sand or plane the edges until they become straight and smooth.

Thirdly, use the dovetail sides to protect the saw at the right angle in order to cut the dovetail groove.

The fourth step is to chisel out the groove and set the dovetail until it gradually slides in and fits well.

Lastly, you now have a completed sliding dovetail. The sliding dovetail can be used to create a leg joint on a work chair that becomes tight as more loads are released on it.

Dado Groove: A groove joint is always used to take hold of the ends of shelf boards to make them stronger. Also, it can be used to catch chair seats on legs, as well as catch splines between boards. It is useful anywhere you want to keep a board from twisting or bending or even make a stronger joint that will carry more load.

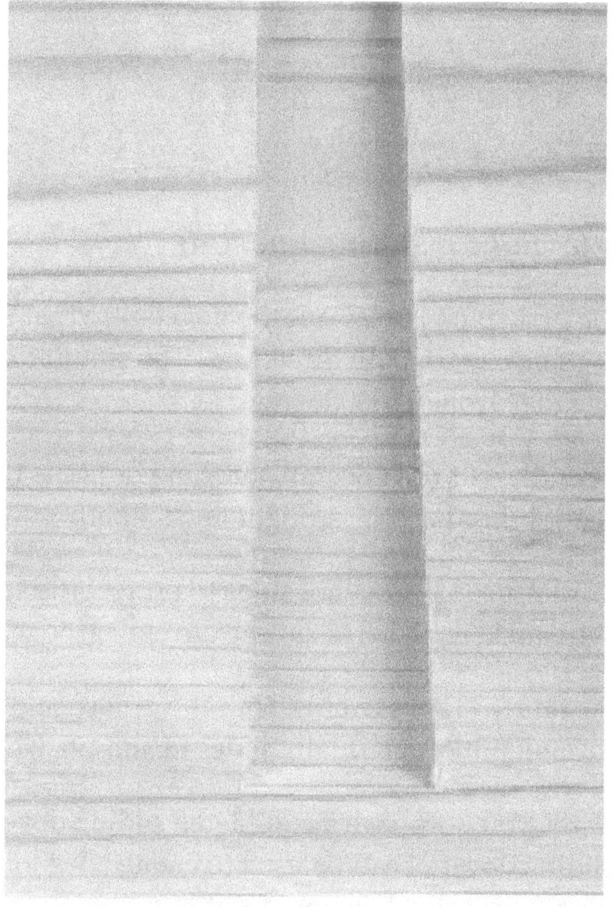

How to make a dado groove

Layout the groove, marking it 0.125-0.5-inch deep, based on how much load it can carry.

Now, clamp a square-cut block to the board to keep your cut in a perpendicular direction.

Saw both sides, hammer, and chisel down to the bottom line.

Complete the dado groove. However, a very simple way to cut the dado groove is to use a table saw with a dado blade.

Dowel Joint: Dowels come in various sizes and can be used to join boards side to side to create workbench countertops, chair or stool seats, and larger shelves. Apart from that, dowels can also be used at the end of a board to incorporate them into an upright for shelves.

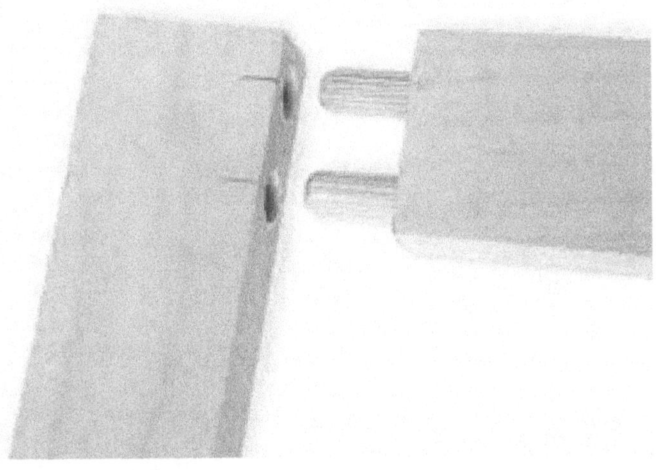

How to make a dowel

Half-inch to three-quarter-inch dowels connect the boards together and are held together by 0.25-inch lock dowels.

Since dowels are usually dry and wood tends to be somehow wet, they usually swell up and stay in place without glue. So, you may call it a permanent joint that will not break easily. However, you will have to drill out the lock dowels to break or separate it apart.

Chapter Summary

Every woodworking project requires the correct wood, and tools to handcraft the best possible finished item. In the next chapter, the wood that Japanese craftsmen select and prefer will be explored. The traditional tools used by the shokunin will also be described with examples of how they are used in practice creating the joinery explained in this chapter.

Chapter Three:
Japanese Wood And Tools

The Japanese's respect and admiration for nature is a core theme within Japanese carpentry, in culture and methods. The wood chosen for building and furniture-making is selected for its specific qualities, appearance and symbolism. In this chapter, the types of wood predominantly used in Japanese carpentry will be explored.

As the islands within the Japanese archipelago feature an abundance of forests, wood was the dominant material used in ancient building methods. In this area of the world, there are native tree species, and the Shokunin discovered which of these species were most suited to different types of projects.

The skills of these craftsmen also encompassed a deep understanding of how each of these species of woods would behave when transformed into lumber. Over centuries of practice, the shokunin cultivated knowledge of how many factors would affect the wood, such as climate, location and position of the tree within its environment.

There are several species of tree that the Shokunin favored and are still used heavily today. These are Japanese Cedar (Sugi), Japanese Red Pine (Akamatsu), and—the most popular and respected—

the Japanese Cypress (Hinoki). These different woods have traditionally been used for specific types of objects in buildings or furniture.

Japanese Cedar

The Japanese Cedar is the national tree of Japan and is often planted around temples and shrines. This is a very large evergreen tree that can reach 230 feet in height and 13 feet in trunk diameter. The bark is a deep, reddish-brown color, and peels in vertical strips. The leaves are spiraled and needle-shaped. The Cedar prefers a forest in a warm, moist climate with well-drained soil.

The Japanese Cedar produces a fragrant timber that is soft with a low density. In building, this wood is found to be particularly weather repellent and resistant to insects and decay. The color is a warm pink with an attractive grain pattern that ages well.

This tree is popular in many types of Japanese construction due to its versatility. The strong, yet light, wood is easy to cut. For these reasons, Cedar is used for furniture-making and other indoor projects, such as paneling and pillars. If buried for aging, the wood turns a beautiful green that is coveted and increases its value.

Japanese Red Pine

The Japanese Red Pine grows throughout Asia and the southeast of Russia. This tree is popular for both timber and as an important ornamental feature for gardens in Japan. The Red Pine is a slender, tall tree that can reach up to 114 feet in height. The needle-shaped leaves are green but can turn yellowish seasonally. The tree prefers well-drained, slightly acidic soil in full sunlight.

The Red Pine's heartwood is a light reddish-brown in color, and the sapwood is a much paler yellow. The wood's grain is straight and linear with an even texture. With a high resin content so it is slightly oily to touch, this wood is lightweight, strong and resistant to rotting.

The Red Pine was traditionally used in bridge construction, due to its unlikelihood to rot over time in wet conditions. It was also popular in temple building, especially for the roof beams.

Japanese Cypress

The Japanese Cypress tree is native to central Japan. It is cultivated by the Japanese for its high-quality wood for timber and ornamental properties. It is worthy to mention that many variations have been bred for differences in size, branch spread and leaf style. It is a slow-growing tree that can reach 115 feet in height and around 3 feet in trunk diameter. The leaves are long and green with blunt tips.

The timber from Japanese Cypress has a pleasant lemon scent and is a light pinkish brown. The grain is straight and beautifully rich. The Cypress dries quickly, which reduces warping, is durable over vast amounts of time and is resistant to rotting.

The Cypress was traditionally used in many building capacities, importantly the construction of temples, shrines and palaces. This versatile timber was also utilized for furniture-making, notably for baths due to its fragrant scent. The Cypress was vital within religious practices, used for Shinto ceremonies and purification rituals.

Japanese Cypress is not only valued as a great building material, but it is also mentioned in ancient Shinto texts as the 'sacred tree'. The wood from the Cypress has many benefits aside from its strength and durability.

All trees emit a substance called phytoncide, a heady aroma with the function of repelling insects and bacteria. The phytoncide scent released by the Japanese Cypress is incredibly pleasant and also causes positive physiological responses in humans. Exposure to this scent can lower blood pressure, improve immunity, have a calming effect, and aid the heart rate and nervous system. The extracted oil from the Cypress has antibacterial properties utilized for the treatment of MRSA (Methicillin-resistant Staphylococcus aureus).

Cypress wood contains aromatic compounds called terpenes, known to absorb toxic substances, such as formaldehyde. The use of Japanese Cypress for buildings has the added benefit of controlling ticks, preventing insect infestation and molds. The Cypress has enormous benefits within temples and homes creating a harmonious and safe environment for residents and visitors. For this reason, it has become common practice for some modern Japanese construction companies to infuse tatami (rice straw) floors, flooring plywood and wallpaper with Cypress oil.

Due to the continuous demand for the Japanese Cypress over the centuries, and the length of time required for the trees to reach a harvestable size for building materials, the production of logging forests have been pushed to the limits. It is part of Shinto belief practices that the many shrines all over the country must be removed and rebuilt every 20 years to please the spirits they are attributed to. This practice symbolizes religious renewal and is a vital part of traditional culture. The rebuilding of these shrines requires 10,000 Cypress trees each 20-year cycle, but the trees take 400 years to grow to the necessary height and size to accomplish these projects.

Mass deforestation in Japan and environmental damage have added to the increasing loss of viable Cypress. The International Union for the Conservation of Nature has listed the Japanese Cypress as 'near threatened'. This could raise the demand for the wood, as the limited availability will define it as a luxury material. The Kiso Valley is home to the last sizable Hinoki forests left in Japan. These forests are managed by the forestry agency, which has begun conservation efforts to manage the number of large trees allowed to be felled each year. These measures are also intended to protect the forest's ecosystem.

Japanese Carpentry Tools:

The distinct woodworking joints of Japanese joinery are created with handheld tools that can be traced back to China in origin. Japanese tools are crafted from very hard steel that are high in carbon content. The edges for cutting are sharpened to an exceptional keenness that can deliver an incredible smoothness in cuts and plane work.

The immense sharpness of the bladed tools means that they are delicate and require practice. Too much force or incorrect use can lead to the breaking of the fine points and edges. The success of any tool in practice lies within the physical relationship of the human and the tool. Habits of movement need to be developed and practiced before the best results can be achieved. Traditionally, Japanese carpenters practice and train for years as apprentices to hone their skills before earning full responsibilities in their profession.

The principles of Japanese carpentry tools are the same as western tools. There are axes, and saws, and chisels for cutting, planes for refining, boring tools for creating holes, and so on. However, the shapes, sizes, materials and methods vary, as these tools have been developed without western influence for the specific techniques unique to Japanese construction.

In this section, Japanese joinery tools will be described and their uses explained.

Japanese Saw (Nokogiri)

The Japanese saw differs from standard western sawing methods in that the Japanese cut on the saw's pull stroke rather than the push stroke. This means that the blade is designed thinner than western saws. These saws have two main kinds of cutting teeth, the crosscut style (yokobiki), and rip style (tatebiki). These two types of teeth are used in single-edged saws and combined for one type of saw called the ryoba (duel edge). There are different types of saws for performing different tasks.

- **Douzuki**: When saws are made with a stiffening back piece, they are suitable for cutting finer joinery designs; these are called douzuki (attached trunk).

- **Osae-biki**: Saws used for flush cutting pegs without marring the wood's surface are called osae-biki (press cut saw), the teeth of this saw have no set to one or both sides.

- **Azebiki**: Saws for cutting in confined areas are azebiki (ridge saw), this saw is short and round, and has both crosscut and rip teeth.

Japanese Plane (Kanna)

The Japanese plane usually resembles a wooden block (dai) featuring a laminated steel blade, a sub-blade, and a securing pin. The main blade is fixed into position with abutments cut into the sides of the dai. This is a similar method to western planes, although these usually feature a wooden wedge that can be tapped down to position the blade. In Japanese planes, the support bed for the blade is convex rather than a flat surface. The blade is tapered in width and thickness. It can be adjusted from the side to achieve a uniform shaving thickness.

Like Japanese saws, planes are also operated using a pulling motion as opposed to the western pushing method. Carpenters often work in a seated position, using their body weight for more force.

Japanese Chisel (Nomi)

Japanese chisels are made from laminated steel of varying strength depending on the intended use. The angle for beveling also varies depending on the type of chisel, with angles ranging from 20 to 35 degrees. Mortising and heavy chisels utilize a steeply angled blade, whereas paring chisels have shallower blades. Many of the woods used in Japanese carpentry are soft, therefore the chisels are made with this in mind, and less force is required to achieve the desired results.

There are many different types of chisel used in Japanese carpentry. These include striking chisels, heavy timber chisels and slicks. There is a range of other specialist chisels used for exact tasks in construction and furniture-making.

Japanese Gimlet (Kiri)

A Japanese gimlet is a tool used for boring holes via a rotating blade tip. There are three types of gimlet differentiated by the structure of the tip and how it rotates.

- **Momigiri**: This gimlet rotates in a backward and forward motion. It is held between the palms and rotated, alternating between left and right. The handle is traditionally made from Japanese Hinoki or Japanese white pine and is long and tapered. There are various variations of momigiri with different amounts of prongs forming the cutting tip.

- **Bourutogiri**: This gimlet works on the same principle as a screw. The cutting blade is diagonal and wood shavings are ejected as the tip is turned. The handle forms a T-shape that is gripped with both hands and turned.

- **Kurikogiri**: This is also known as a brace. It consists of a sharp head, attached to a U-shaped iron rod. Different types of cutting heads can be fitted into the chuck via a regulating screw. The round part of the handle remains steady, whilst the middle of the handle is rotated. The kurikoguri is suitable for boring larger holes.

Japanese Hammer (Genno or Gennoh):

There are several purposes for Japanese hammers. One is used in conjunction with the chisel for cutting refined shapes. Some hammers are used for positioning hand blades, some for removing nails, and some for tapping out laminated hardened steel from the base of chisels and plane blades.

Marking and Measuring Tools

There are various tools used in Japanese carpentry and joinery for measuring and marking wood. An important part of any woodworking project is accuracy, and these tools are necessary for ensuring that the placing and size of each cut is correct and that precision is achieved.

The inkpot is used to mark long straight lines. The process involves a thread tied to a rounded piece of wood that has a needle attached at its end. The other end of this thread is passed through the inkpot via a small opening and through the depression containing the ink. Then, the thread is wound around a spool. The ink is stored soaked in silk wadding. The thread is held in the left hand whilst the needle is fixed onto the required place on the wood's surface.

The inkpot is then moved away from the needle until enough thread is unreeled for the correct length of the line. The thread is pulled until tight, then released, marking the wood. Other tools used for marking include the kiridashi (marking knife), sumisashi (bamboo pen), kebiki and kinshiro (traditional single and multi-blade marking gauges).

For measuring, traditional carpenters did not have the same methods as modern tapes and rules. They used a carpenter's square. This is a framing square marked with several units of measurement on each side. The square can be used for measuring and marking lines and marks for cutting that will be accurate with each repetition of a shape.

In Japanese joinery, accurate measuring and marking are crucial as each joining piece of wood must be exact for the join to be strong. Each tool plays an important part in creating the ideal shapes, and each tool must be in great condition to achieve a perfect and accurate join.

For cutting tools' blades, a similar process is used for forging samurai swords. Japanese steel is highly refined and strong. A very hard blade metal is welded to a softer piece of metal in a forge. The softer base metal is intended to absorb shock and prevent the harder, more brittle metal from breaking. This technique creates a harder chisel than western models. This also means a finer edge that is difficult to source outside of Japan.

Blades of Japanese planes and chisels have a unique distinguishable feature, a hollow in their flat side called the ura. The purpose of this hollow ensures a high degree of flatness during sharpening, as when the flat side is polished, it is making contact only with the stone on either side of its width. This enhances the precision of cuts made with the chisel and ensures the plane has smooth contact with the wedge and even support. This hollow also reduces the amount of metal needed and reduces friction as the chisel is driven into the wood.

The sharpening process of these blades by Japanese carpenters typically involves three or more whetstones. The carpenter progresses from the roughest stone and ending at the finest. When practicing Japanese joinery, it is vital to maintain the sharpness of the bladed tools and replace the blades of saws to ensure that the cuts made are accurate, and the most is being made of the elegant tools used for these processes.

Chapter Summary

Really, chapter two was the premise of this book. It discussed everything you need to know about joints as stated below:

- The different types of joints.

- A simple and effective way of making joints without using nails and screws.

- Special characteristics of different joints and their specialized uses.

- Joints that don't need any specialized tools and how to make them, and many more.

In the following chapter, we'll learn the process of Japanese joinery in its entirety. Come along as we embark on this tour.

Chapter Four: The Process of Japanese Joinery

The process of Japanese joinery is based on a learning system that involves many years of commitment and determination of any individual interested in the craft. The secrets of the Japanese joinery and woodworking craft were passed down from Master to apprentice through an oral tradition. These secrets are the same as the technical skills of woodworking. They varied greatly from one carpentry school to another.

It was not until the Edo period that some of the hidden technical skills of the Japanese joinery craft began to be recorded in writing by government officials as a means to establish a standard for residential construction. Still, the knowledge of Japanese joinery was not recorded much even with the intervention of the government.

Unlike many other traditional joinery methods, Japanese joinery has recently remained a secretive craft amongst closely knitted carpentry families in Japan. The complicated joints are made with exactness and skill, deploying various end, corner and intermediate joints to meticulously cancel the effects of loads and torsions.

Components fit together like puzzle pieces to produce intelligent structures. Of course, these combinations are known to be amongst some of the longest-surviving structures even still today. Japanese joinery does not depend on permanent fixtures, such as screws, nails and glues. Rather, joints are firmly held together using interlocking connections and depend on material properties to withstand forces and pressure.

How the Japanese carpenter uses Japanese joinery

Japanese carpentry is popular for its ability to create everything from temples to houses to tea houses to furniture without the use of any nails, screws or power tools. This is done through a process called joinery.

Also, Japanese carpentry has a long history from many centuries ago. Construction in the western world tends to separate an architect/designer from the constructor. However, it's not so in Japan, as the carpenter is also the architect.

In the same vein, Japanese carpentry looks simple and purposeful. The finished pieces' beauty matches development with nature. Nevertheless, the techniques beneath the structures are different and intricate, as they use joinery ingenuity to construct buildings that do not depend on nails or bolts.

Japanese Joinery

Joinery is a construction process that involves the creation of interlocking joints. In a nutshell, these joints carefully join selected pieces of wood together firmly. Traditional Japanese craftsmanship is evident in many of the different traditional inns or small hotels located in Japan.

Japanese wood joints form the basis of the country's great temples, houses and cabinetry. They're designed with joinery techniques that are still being studied by contemporary architects today. These designs are able to use joinery that does not require steel nails, but still forms sturdy internal structures to big buildings while presenting elegant visual constructions within the room's ceilings.

Traditional Japanese aesthetics included wood as the major building material for a number of reasons. The nation was gifted with a myriad of timber resources and the light weight of the material made it a favorable alternative to stone or brick, as earthquakes regularly destroyed the country's coast and rural areas. With the threat of earthquakes in mind, the joints had also been designed to be able to withstand the jolts with the flexibility that other rigid construction materials could not offer.

These joints matched the Japanese minimal aesthetic that had been inspired by early Taoism, but this simplicity was a deceiving perception. The complicated nature of Japanese joinery has been described most times as *geometry meets nature.* It is indeed an *exceptionally well-thought-out process* of incorporating wood pieces to form stable structures. Japanese architecture was never too far from nature, and the character it added to traditional buildings is an obvious contrast to the westernized monoliths that stand tall in the nation's urban areas today.

Many Japanese carpenters have remained loyal to the old crafts, continuing to use traditional joinery techniques in contemporary furniture and woodwork projects. The country manages to produce supreme joinery and woodwork techniques as well as woodwork tools by honoring the craft of past centuries. This same honor also goes to Japan's lauded architecture design.

Fortunately, the processes and secrets are now easier to understand, meaning the advanced techniques have become accessible for even non-professionals attempting DIY projects.

Joinery in small-scale projects

Although dovetailing is one of the techniques in Japanese joinery, it is effective at joining pieces of furniture together. Also, it is relatively a new technique that is more suitable for small-scale projects. It is traditionally right in Japan for carpenters to perform the dual roles of being both architects and home-builders. But, if Japanese carpenters want to handle big projects, what do you think they can do?

Joinery in large-scale projects

There is a need for master Japanese carpenters to utilize advanced techniques for large-scale projects, such as tea houses, shrines and homes. In essence, these advanced techniques make way for ample load-bearing weight. They also allow for a major construction project without the use of common western materials, such as screws or nails.

However, there's one stark disadvantage here. Japanese carpentry is a difficult skill to learn and master. Besides that, it also needs a larger investment in time. So, it is quite hard to join these pieces together using Japanese joinery. Nevertheless, it is a testament to the mastery that these carpenters possess together with the long Japanese history of many years in intricate woodworking.

The Four Types of Japanese Carpenters

Japanese carpenters adopt the same mode of operation. However, they can be divided into four different types of professions. There are three major factors that control the way these carpenters are separated into different types of carpentry, namely:

- Their level of experience with various forms of joinery.

- The wide variety of joints they create.

- The tools they apply in the creation of joints.

The four distinct similar but different professions are explained below:

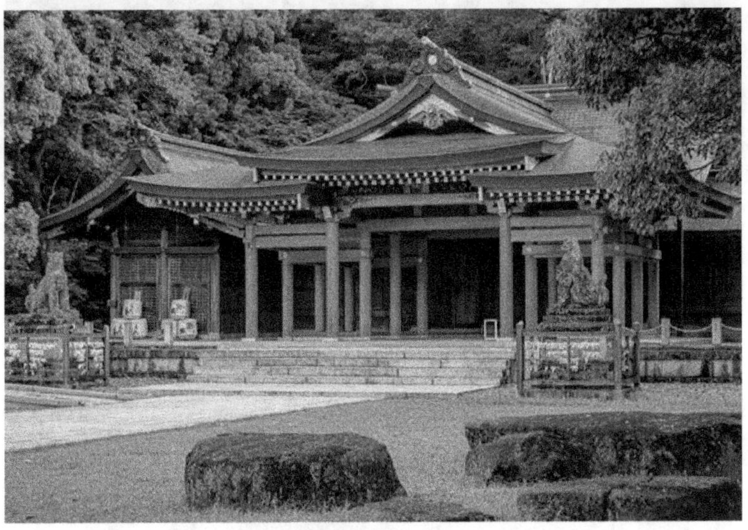

1. Miyadaiku (Shrine Carpenters)

Here, the carpenters are engaged in the building and construction of Japanese shrines, as well as temples. They make use of well-detailed joints to construct powerfully structured and highly long-lasting structures. As a result, these buildings are commonly found among the world's longest-surviving wooden structures.

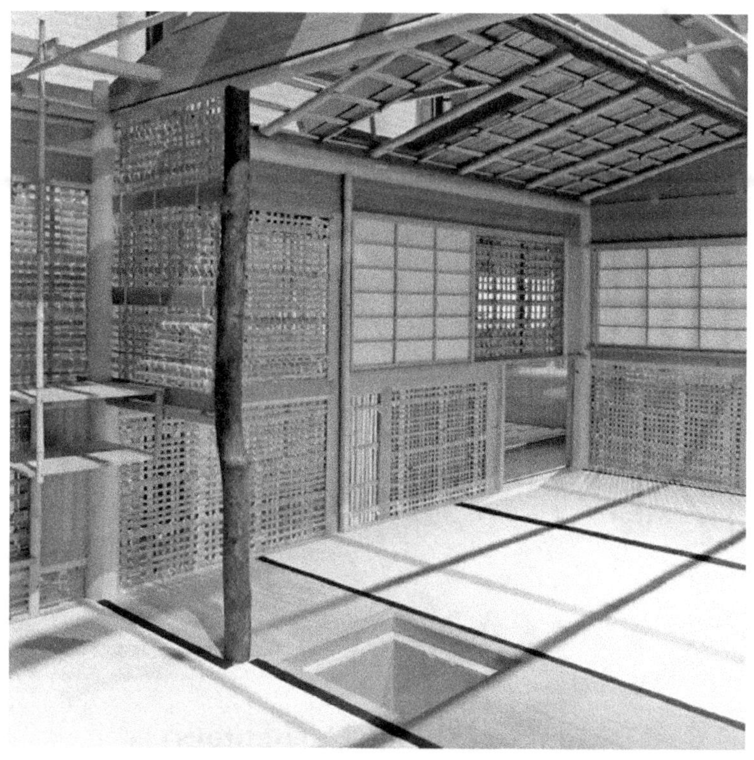

2. Sukiya-daiku (Tea-House Makers)

These breeds of carpenters are more popular for their particularly delicate and aesthetic constructions. Typically, they engage in the construction of treehouses and residential-type structures, such as staircases and window frames.

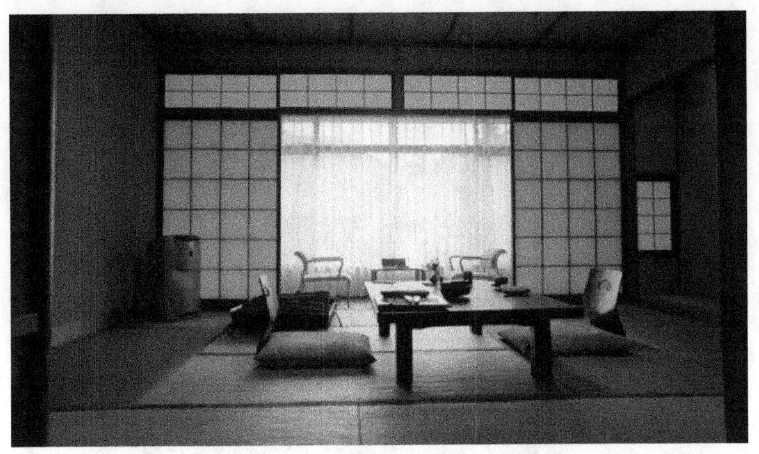

3. Tateguya (Interior Carpenters)

The tateguya are carpenters who take care of interior finishing work. These people are interior finishing experts who build shōji (Japanese sliding doors). Furthermore, they also create carved, small wooden wall decorations that are known as *Ranma*.

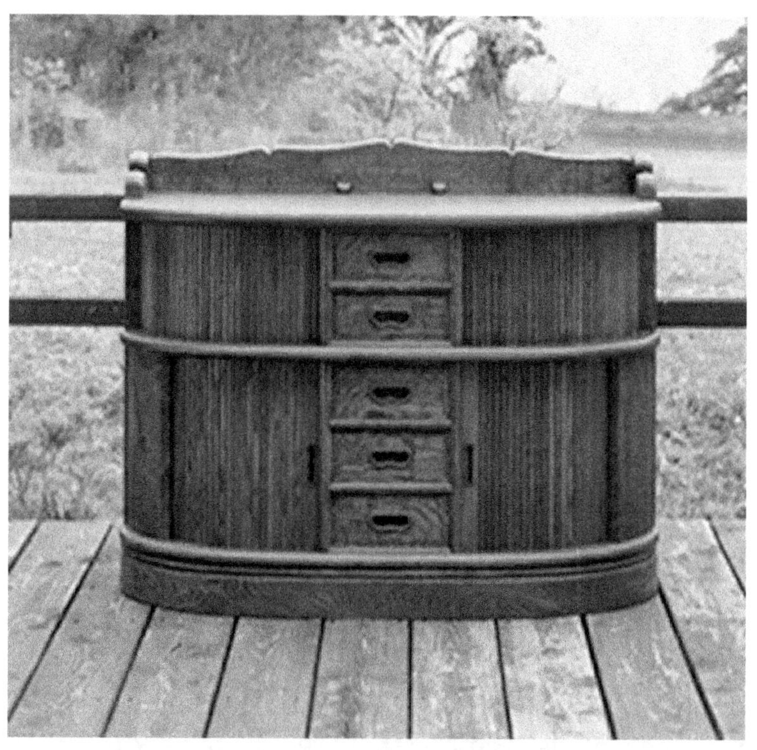

4. Sashimono-shi (Furniture-Makers)

These furniture-makers are similar to the tateguya. The only difference is that they create more general-purpose furniture, such as chairs, sofas, cabinets and more.

Although, it is not always the case for a Japanese carpenter to work outside the realms of their specific skill or profession, it does happen. There are carpentry workshops in Japan that will perform two separate skill sets. Mostly, the *miyadaiku* and *sukiya-daiku* are usually the two such professions.

Japanese carpenters are artists, indeed. Their joinery strategies, as well as a deep appreciation of sturdy woods, such as the *hinoki*, make them unique in their skills. As such, their skills are something that has been sharpened and perfected for more than a millennium, and they prove their worth. It is admirable to carefully observe Japanese carpenters in action and to see the final product. To this end, this book and many videos, as well as websites available around the Internet, can help you learn more.

The various processes involved in the selection of wood

How do you get started with Japanese joinery? Are there processes to follow and what are the conditions you must meet in order to select the hinoki for your construction and joinery projects?

Well, you're not far from the destination. Here you are!

Now, to go from the selection of wood to the completion of a project involves a series of working processes. These procedures, each of which requires the highest level of craftsmanship, jointly influence the final outcome of the product. However routine some of these processes may become, the carpenter will still deeply consider and carefully judge and apply the habits acquired through many years of practice.

Here, we'll discuss one crucial woodworking manufacturing process, which is the choice of wood for your project. The choice of timber entails choosing the right wood species for the object to be produced and judging the quality of that wood.

Moreover, the choice of the right wood species, such as hinoki, for a project determines the product's durability, unique features and characteristics. Each of the four distinct carpentry professions has a range of wood species, each of which impacts the economic, aesthetic, technical and symbolic conditions.

Economic conditions are determined by the history and origin of the wood, its availability, quality, and price. Therefore, products meant for daily use are produced from local wood, while sophisticated items, such as utensils for a tea ceremony, are produced from imported or precious indigenous wood.

Technical conditions consider those properties and qualities of wood that make it suitable for the different purposes for which it is required. Some of these properties include weight, moisture content, durability, elasticity and flexibility.

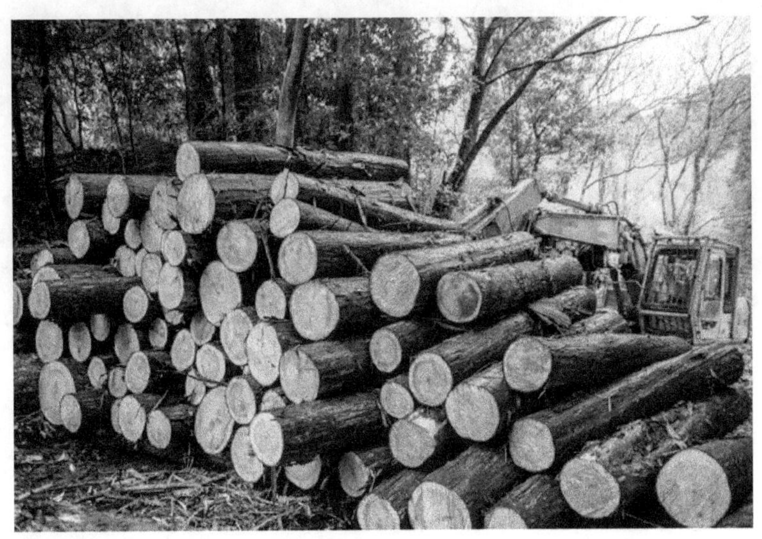

Hinoki – Japanese Cypress

The wood from Japanese Cypress is fragrant as a result of its high oil and resin content. It has a powerful scent that smells like aromas of spicy lemon and sweet, and it produces resinous coniferous notes reminiscent of Pine and Cypress.

Also, the wood is highly expensive and produces exceptional timber as a result of its rich, straight grain and its brilliant rot resistance. It has been used to build castles, as well as palaces, temples, shrines, Noh theatres, and traditional japanese baths (Onsen).

It is also highly sought after as an ornamental tree and can be found in many gardens, parks and shrines. As a beginner in the Japanese joinery profession, you can subscribe to the services of any of the four types of Japanese carpenters to help you source this wood.

Examples of Basic Joinery Process

Before these examples are rolled out, it's important you know that they'll highlight the fundamental processes for basic joinery, helping you to get ready to start your project with ease.

Tongue-and-Groove Joint: This joint allows for wood shrinkage. Cut a groove in the edge of one piece of the wood. Also, cut a tongue on the other wood piece to fit into the groove. Get two pieces of finely textured wood of equal size, length and thickness.

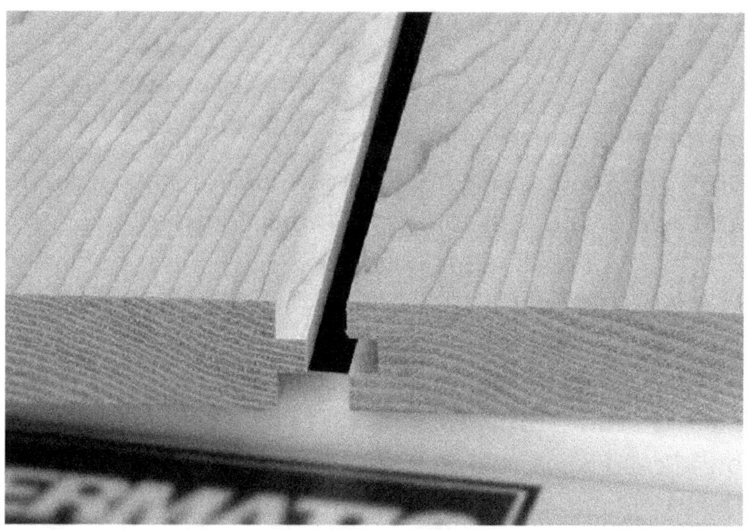

The first step is to make a non-through cut through the two mating workpieces of the tongue-and-groove joint by not allowing the saw blade to go all the way through the wood.

Turn on your table saw and run the wood through to cut the first face. This will create a *rabbet* down the edge to form half the tongue. Move on to the next stage by flipping the workpiece end-for-end. Repeat the cut on the same edge of the opposite face, to produce the finished tongue.

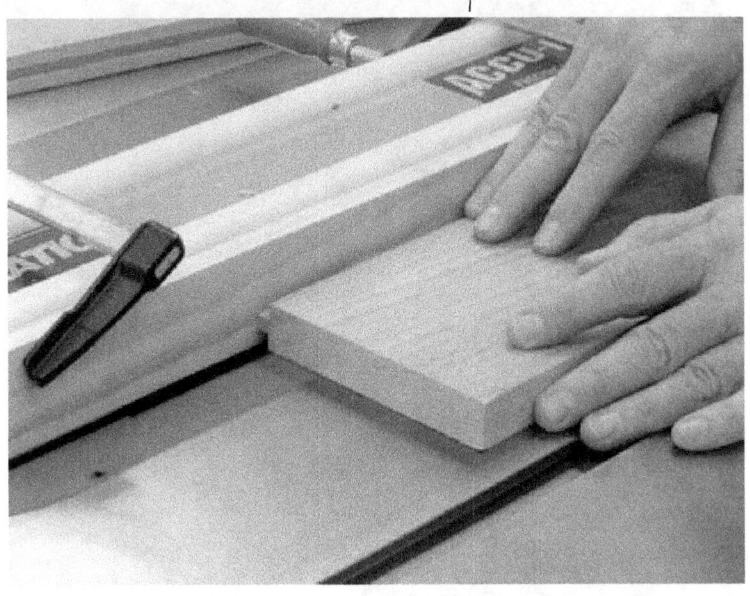

Check the fit of the resulting joint. How? Simply by slipping one workpiece into the other.

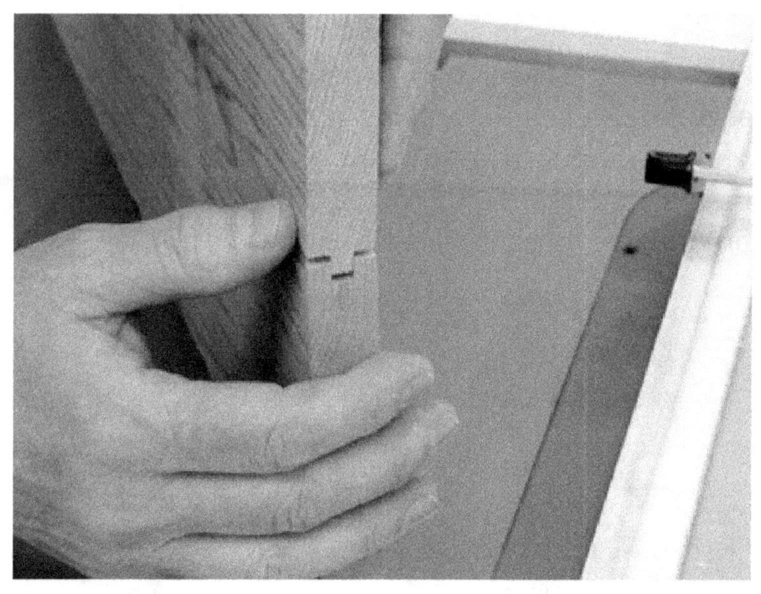

Slip the tongue firmly into the groove and clamp up the assembly.

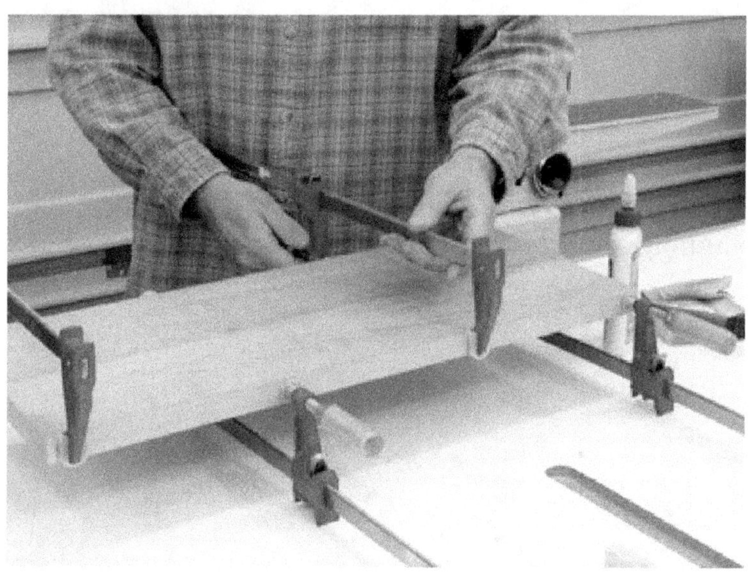

Chapter Summary

- How the Japanese carpentry industry uses Japanese joinery;

- There are four types of Japanese carpenters;

- There are various processes involved in the selection of wood; and

- An example of basic joinery was demonstrated.

All of the above were talked about in this interesting chapter.

It's now time to build a simple square frame as we proceed to chapter four.

Chapter Five:
Building a Simple Square or Rectangular Frame

Basically, wood joinery refers to joining pieces of wood, timber or lumber together to create other structures. If you're really interested in gaining woodworking skills, take this time out to learn the major strong types of wood joints shown below. After all, the stronger the joints, the more long-lasting the final products.

The unique feature of skilled woodworking is the ability to build tight wood joints. The edges mix seamlessly thereby making two joined pieces look like a single piece. To successfully create most types of wood joints, you'll need to make precise cuts.

It is often a requirement to build simple timber frames in woodwork. Fortunately, there are many simple joints that can be used to create them. Where frames are used, they are often covered with plywood or other man-made boards. When a frame is used, it adds strength to the product. This makes it easier for a relatively thin board to be used, thereby saving on both material and cost.

Building a Simple Frame Using Interlocking Miter Joint

A miter joint is created when two end pieces are cut on angles and fitted together. It is commonly found in the corners of picture frames as well as the upper ends of some styles of doorway casing (trim).

When considering a quality 90-degree mitered corner, the two pieces of wood are cut on opposite 45-degree angles and joined together. In the same vein, when installing trim, the pieces are joined at the seam and then fastened to the framing material on the wall.

However, if you want to create mitered corners for a freestanding object, like a picture frame, the pieces of wood are joined at the joint, using well-constructed dovetail joints that do not require nails and screws to hold them together permanently to each other. Looking at freestanding woodworking projects, nearly all miter joints need both gluing and extra fasteners. But here, we're not going to use any fastener; just handcrafted joints that will go into each other and lock up for life.

Steps to Building the Frame

Step one: Choose frame size and glass

You can use any size of wood for your frames. What really matters is just your taste or preference. You may choose 2" x 2" softwood planed timber for your frames. Maybe your plan is to create nice large frames of different sizes to cover a big wall. You can purchase a piece of glass to fit or use glass from old frames that we all have stashed in some dark corner of the house.

Also, you may as well use an inexpensive diploma frame glass and some small thick glass from old halogen light. If you want to cut the glass, you can use a tile cutter as it will perform a great job. You need to exercise caution here so that you don't cut yourself. Always use safety gloves while performing any cut.

Remember, it is better to adjust the frame to the glass and not the other way.

Step two: Cut the wooden planks

There are two ways to cut 45-degree angles. One cutting option is the manual way, using a 45-degree miter box with a tenon saw. All you have to do is to ensure the blade of the tenon saw is set well straight and at the correct 45-degree angle before cutting. Always test first on scrap wood.

Step three: Decide which molding bit to use for the frame design

There are many ways that you can achieve decorative molding for the frame. You can use a straight bit, a cove bit, a round corner bit and a 45 degree bit. After setting the bit to the right and desired height, as well as the distance from the table fence, ensure you always practice the first cut on a piece of scrap wood to see if the setting and RPM gives you the best finish you want.

When using a straight bit, you should always do the cuts in a few shallow passes. But don't force the wood on the bit in one go, as it might burn the bit and the wood finishing will be very poor.

Another way is to first cut all the frame parts and then run them on the router table or take the full length of wood you want to use. Perform all the moldings before you cut it into the frame size of your choice. Just choose the option that is easier for you.

Step four: Put the piece together

When you're done cutting the frame parts to size, make a dry assembly to know whether the glass fits well. Get the frame parts ready to be put together, then assemble them together, fixing each joint together and mildly hitting the ends of the joints with a small mallet to drive the joints in very well.

Make sure to keep the frame together down on a flat surface. It will prevent a twist that might destroy all your work. Give the frame a light sanding, working up the grit level. Sand the frame properly and clean it well by dusting off the frame and using dye or paint. You can even leave it natural. More so, if you use old pine effect dye, the finished frame will look awesome.

Step five: Create holes for hanging the frame

The aim of using the washer is just to stop the frame from falling, which is unlikely but won't do any harm. Alternatively, you can just drill a hole in the center of the top frame.

You can use a 16mm bit for a shallow hole to fit the washer and 9mm in the inner hole. Lastly, cut a 2mm back support for the glass and close with small pins under each corner of the glass.

Lastly, it is important to highlight here that the miter, which is only slightly stronger than the butt, is used almost exclusively for appearance sake (through burnishing) as the joint hides the exposed end grain of both pieces of wood. This is the standard type for picture frames and small decorative finishes.

With thin wooden boards, the miters can be cut using a handsaw although using a power circular saw with a guide or jig will translate into a more precise cut. However, with a top-quality woodworking project like this one, the methods of joinery are often entirely invisible.

Chapter Summary

This chapter spokemuch on tools and joints. We considered the steps needed to create a simple square frame, how to make joints using proportionate measurements, and the importance of burnishing to create a beautiful product. Now, it's time to move

ahead with a bit of an advanced project, such as
building a step stool.

Chapter Six: Construct a Step Stool

The step stool is simple furniture, but exceptionally multi-functional in nature. A step stool is a useful piece of furniture in homes, warehouses, shops, workshops, libraries, offices, and other working environments, where it is used for convenient access and maintenance jobs. It can help in accomplishing jobs that need to be done at an elevated position.

In this chapter, come along as you'll be shown how to build a step stool using Japanese joinery. This woodworking project is suitable for a novice who is looking for a task requiring hand-cut joinery. Using simple knowledge you've acquired so far about Japanese joinery, this timeless and functional piece of furniture will be a woodworking project you'll enjoy building.

Step one: Get materials for your step stool

Look for a dry piece of construction lumber that has probably been lying idle in your shed, workshop or house for years. Such woods are usually free, hard, dry and won't warp after use for some months. Besides, you'll save yourself money, other resources and effort. But, if you don't have old lumber, you can purchase finished laminated boards.

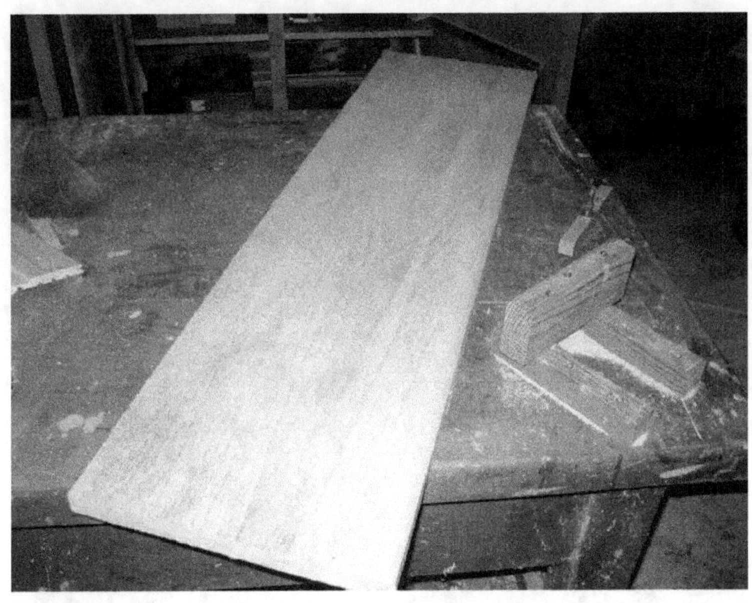

Dimensions for your boards are the following: 47.24 inches in length, 13 inches in width, and 1 inch in thickness. After making the step stool, the dimensions should be 17.7 inches in width, 8.66 inches in length, and the height of the legs is 11.81 inches, respectively. The thickness should remain 1 inch. These measures are not compulsory to use, you can use them as a guide and not a rule.

When using construction lumber, especially the one where you don't know the source, always ensure you check for any metal objects, such as nails, that can injure you or even harm your tools. Try your best to comply with all the safety information on your power tool and use it with care.

Step two: Rip the lumber before cutting

Ripping of lumber involves tearing the big board into smaller strips using a handheld planer or any other tool of your choice and then putting it back together. This will make the board more straight, and it remains so for many years to come.

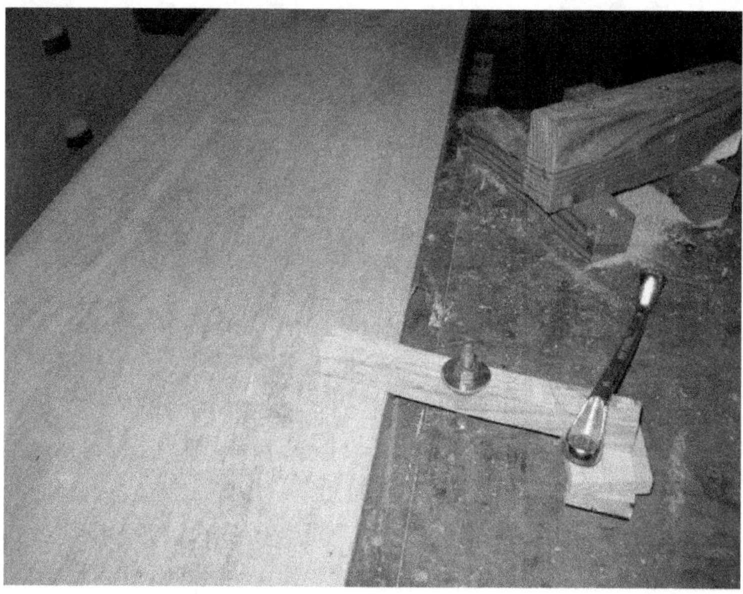

To get a straight board, rip the lumber to 2.2 inches or any measurement of your choice. More so, you'll have to measure out 5 pieces of 2.2 inches lumber, so that 4 pieces go for board while one piece is for connecting the legs of the stool together.

If you have a table saw, that'll be better. If not, use the handheld circular saw. Although it has a poor guide, you can make a simple guide in a matter of minutes and use it. Get a straight piece of wood and attach it to the bottom of a circular saw with screws. You can do this by drilling 2 holes through the circular saw base.

Measure the distance between the glue wood and blade of the saw using a measuring tape. Remember the distance is supposed to be 2.2 inches and must be equal on both sides of the blade in order to have a straight cut.

Also, check the depth of your saw blade and adjust it. It should be slightly more than the board thickness. This will eliminate the incident of a back kick of circular saw, which often happens when the blade is put too low in the wood. Always clamp your wood pieces before working on them.

Step three: Proceed with cutting the board

Now, hold your saw very tight. Gently press the teeth against the board's edge, then cut. Do not stand at the back of the saw when cutting. Instead, stand on the side to ensure that the saw is behind you so that when you lose control and experience a back kick, the saw will not harm you. This is applicable to table saws.

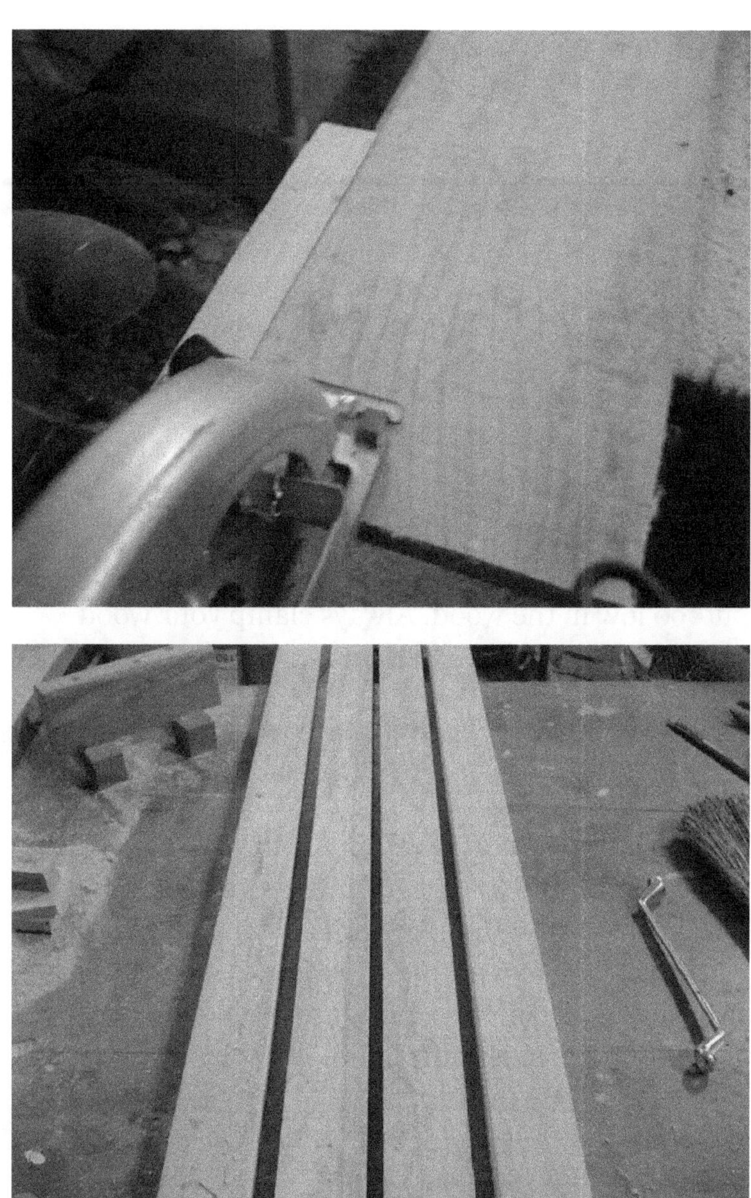

When you're done with the cutting, you'll have 5 pieces of boards, as stated earlier.

Step four: Plane the wood

At this stage, get a handheld planer, as it might be difficult sourcing a table jointer or thickness planer. Adjust the planing depth and plane down each piece of wood. The best approach is to plane the wider sides first and take note of how many times you plane it. This is important to maintain the same thickness of each wood piece and assist in gluing.

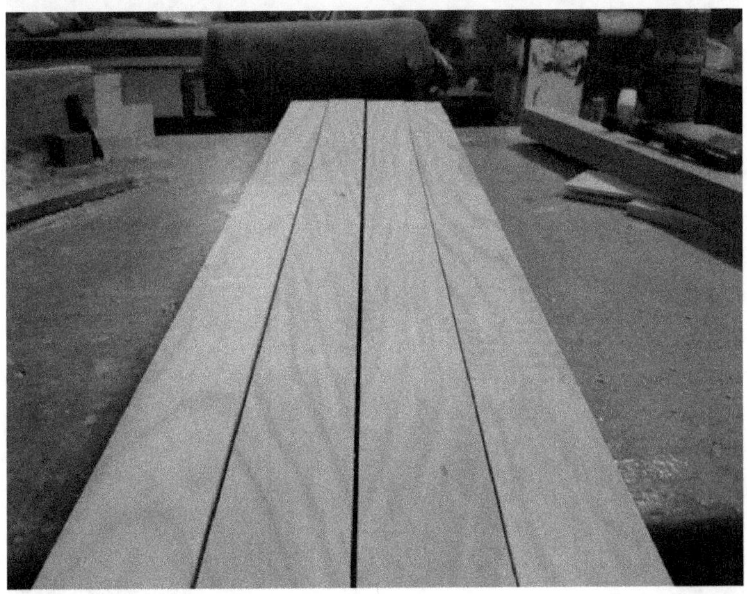

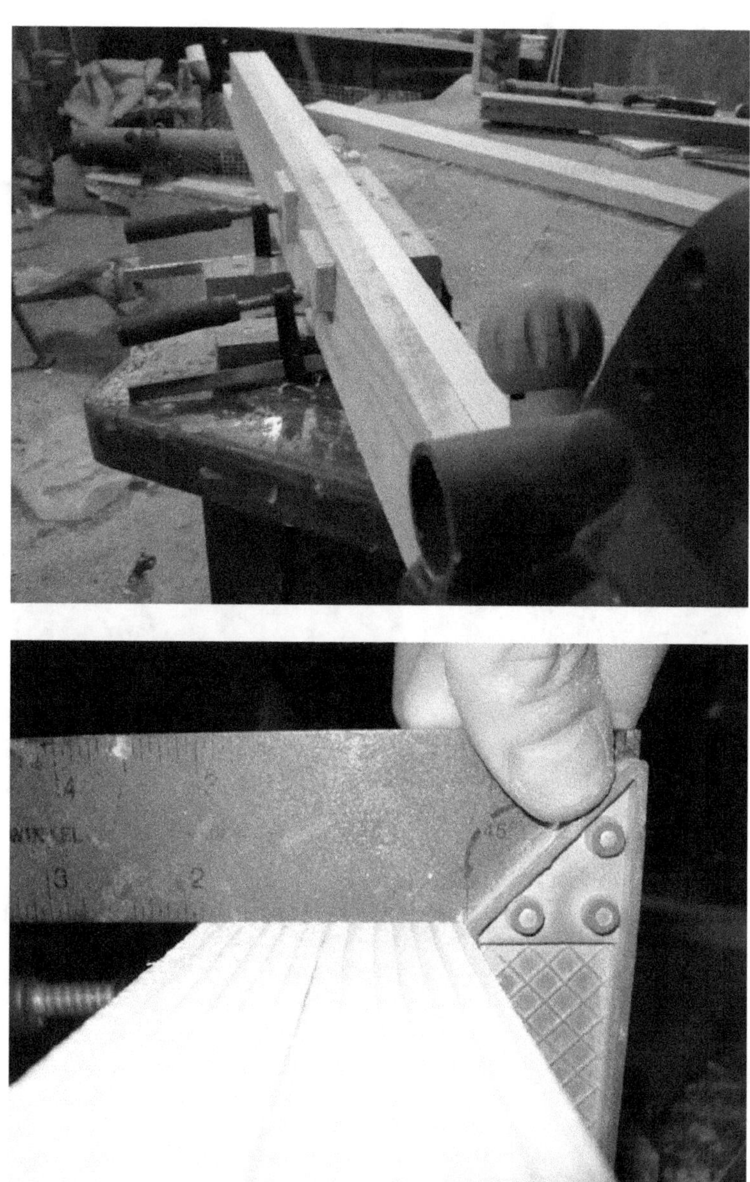

Now, plane the narrow sides, and don't forget to plane them in pairs to keep the pieces squared.

Step five: Put the pieces together

You have to make sure that the wood surfaces are smooth. So, sand narrow parts with 40-grit sandpaper to have an excellent joint. Arrange the pieces, which will be joined, uniformly and equally on all sides.

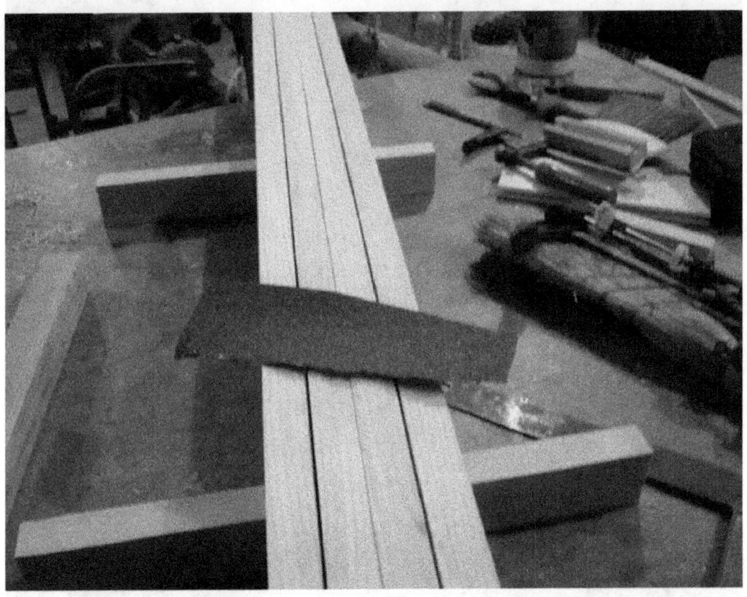

Clamp all the wood pieces together after passing dowel nuts through the narrow parts to make them align well and form the board. Remove excess protrusion from the joints.

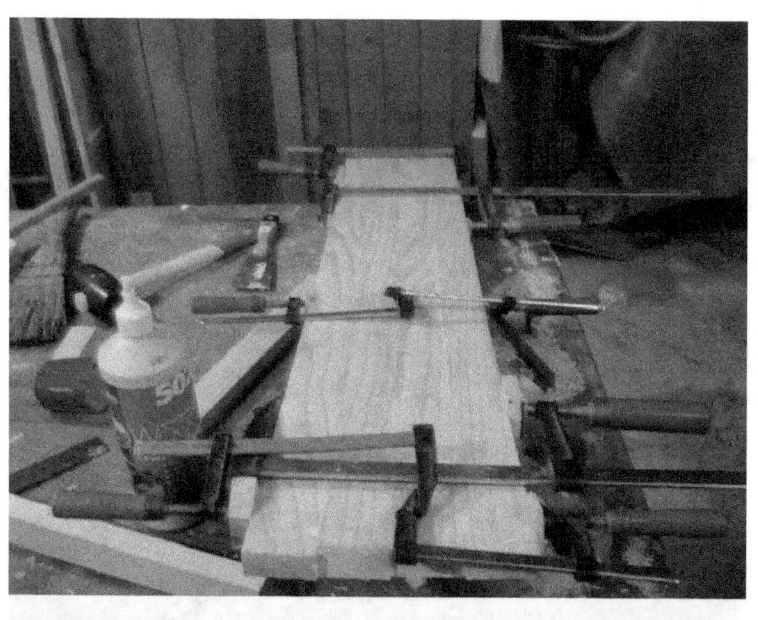

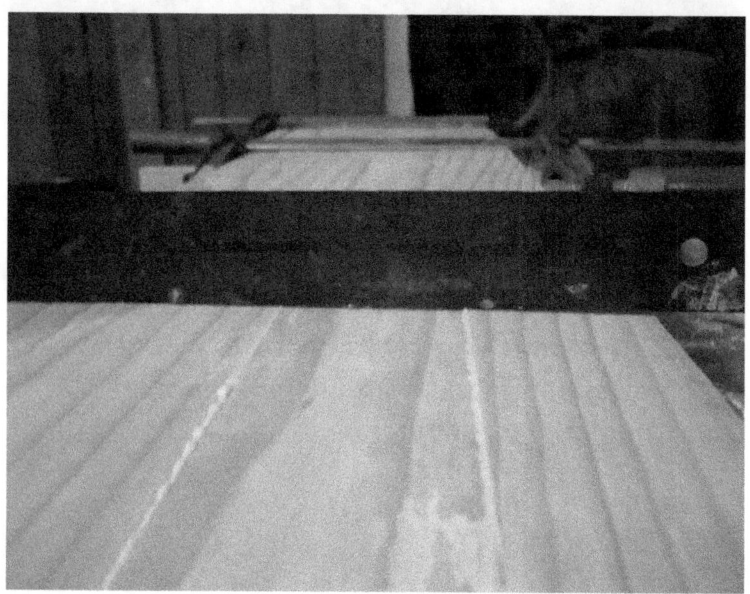

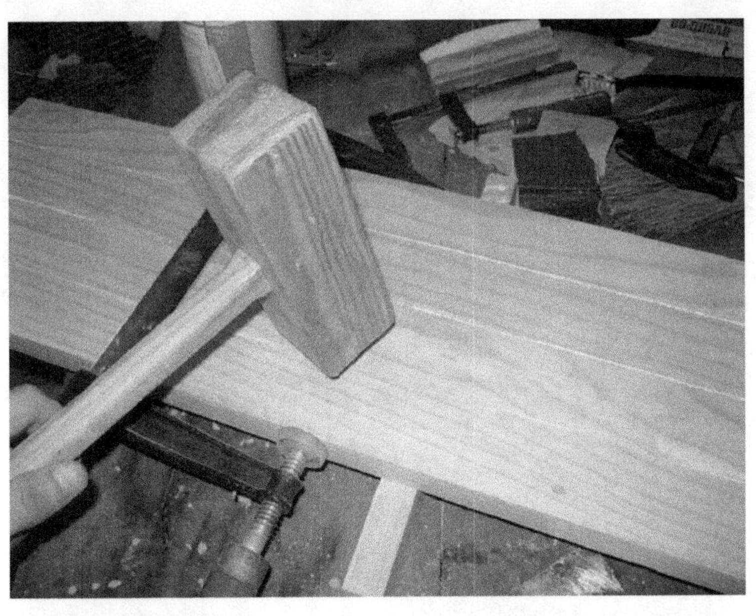

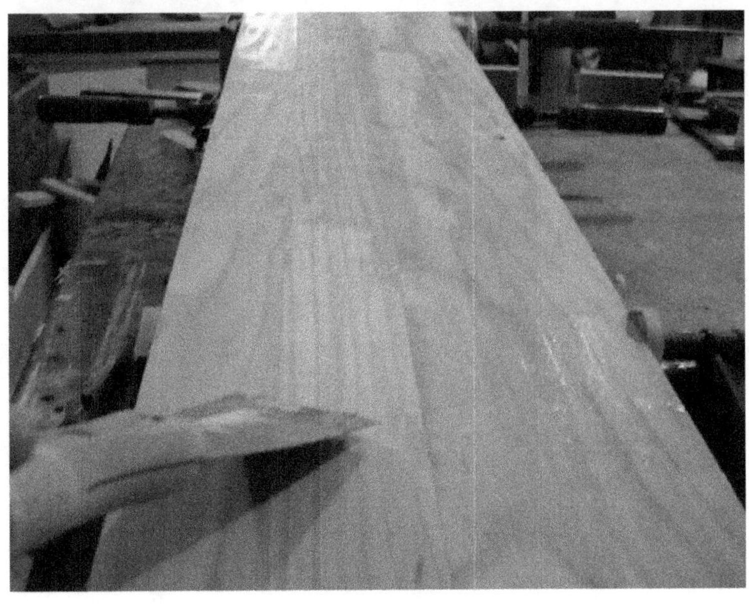

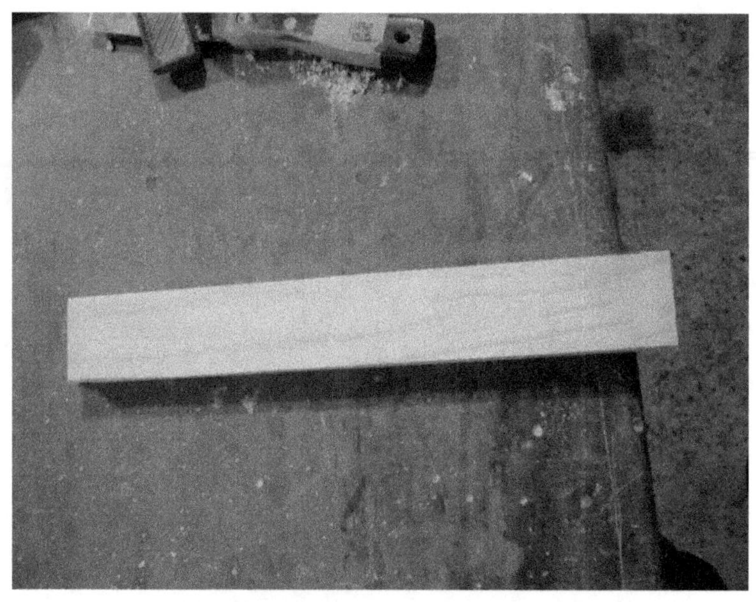

Specifically for the fifth wood piece that will connect the legs of the stool together, cut it to 13.77 inches using a regular hand saw or even any other type of saw. Then, leave the clamped piece to dry.

Step six: Flatten and sand the piece

As soon as you remove the clamp, you should have a board that is strong, nice and elegant. If not so, maybe the board is not flat, especially the edges. So, what will you do?

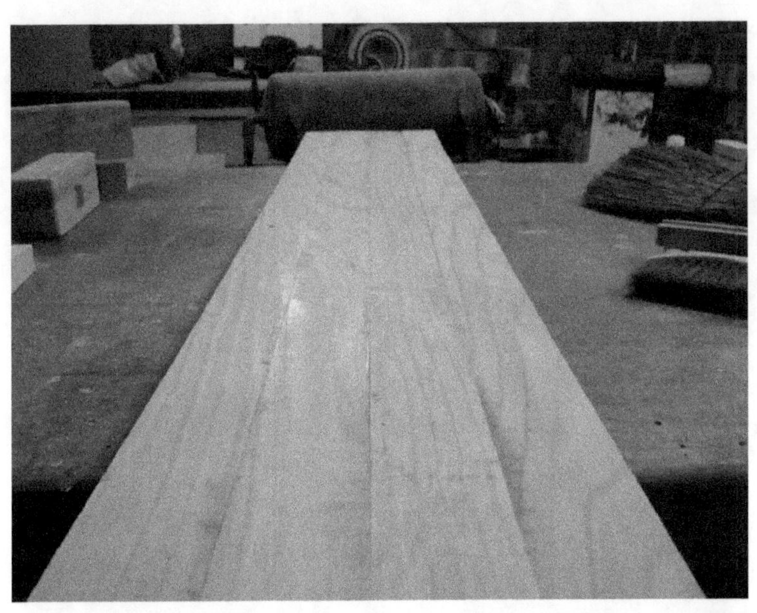

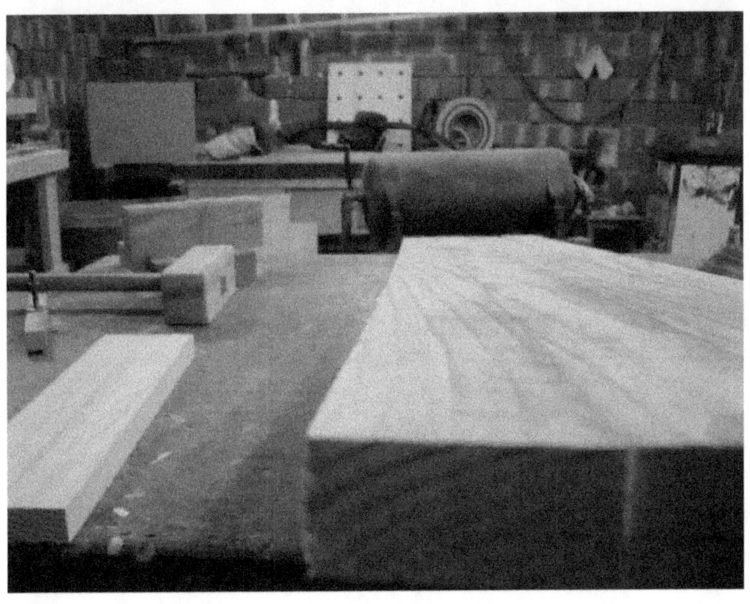

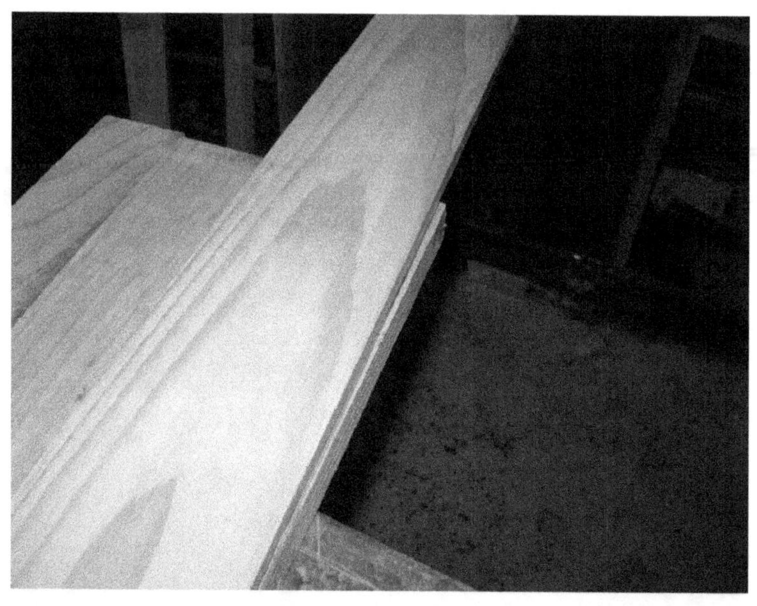

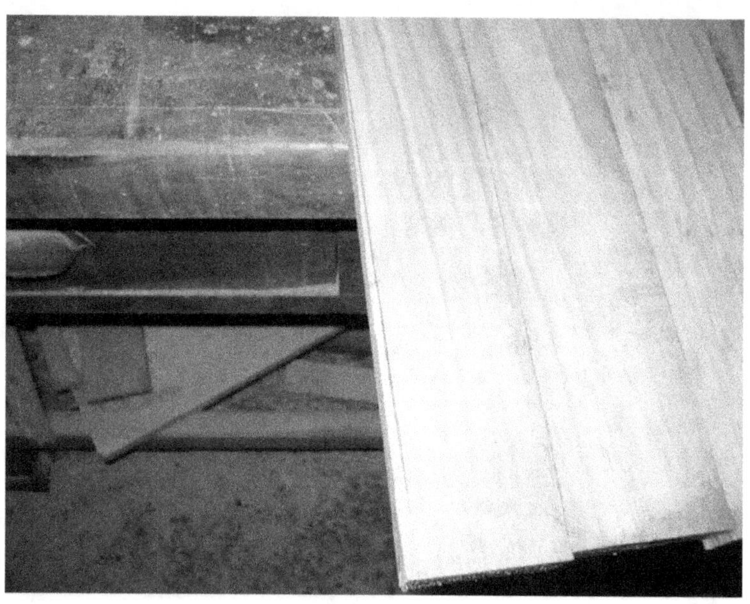

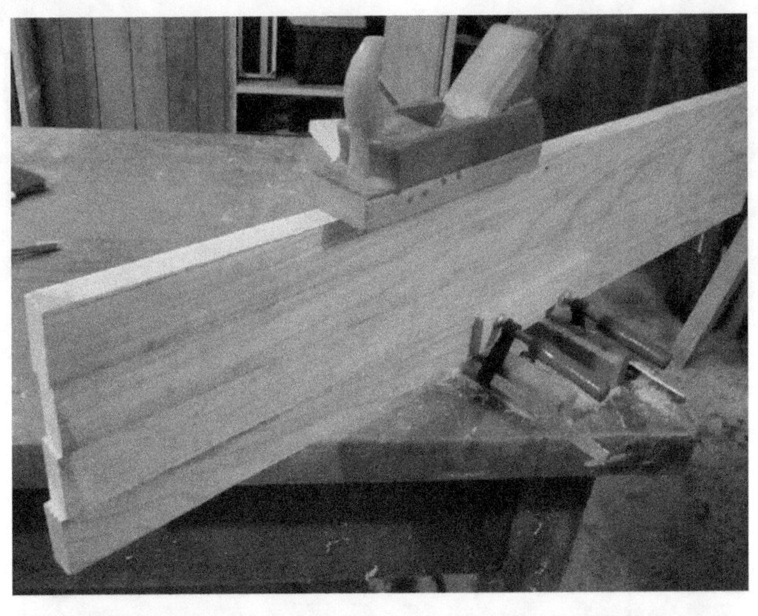

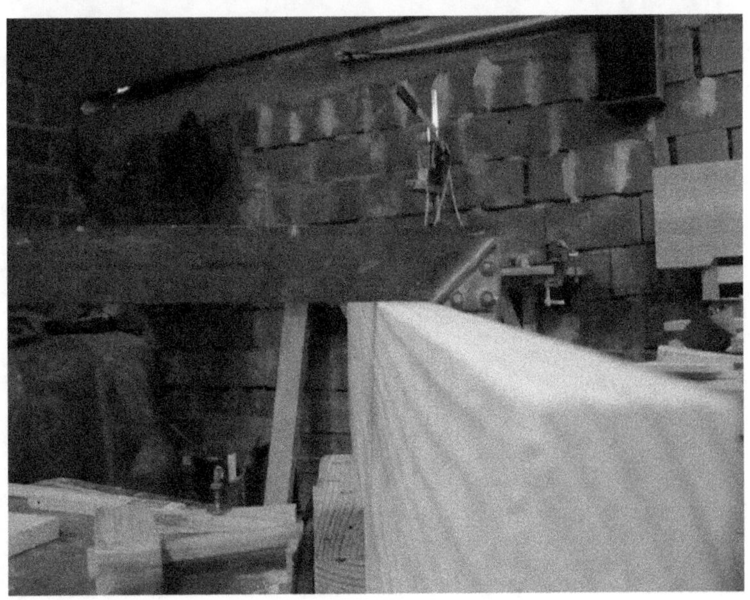

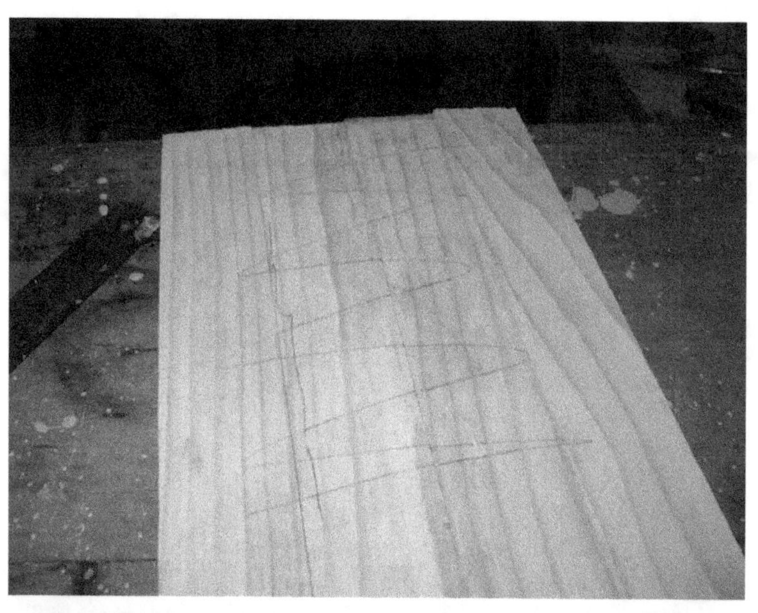

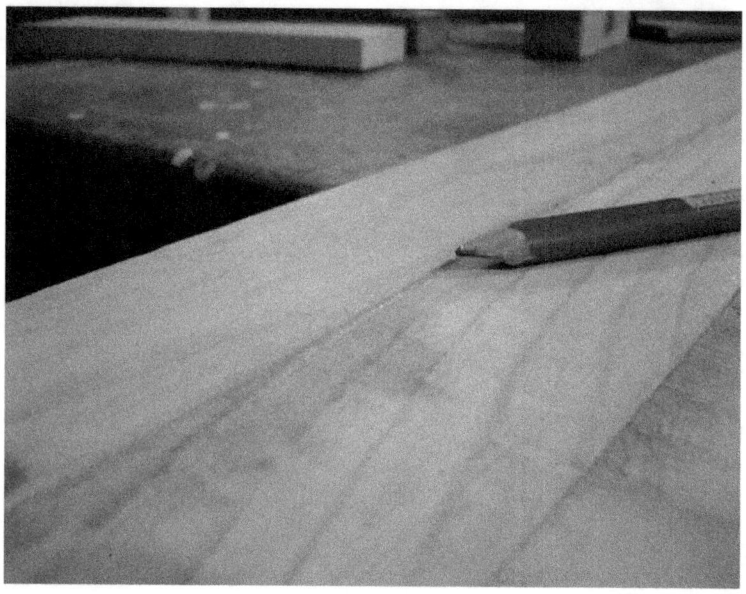

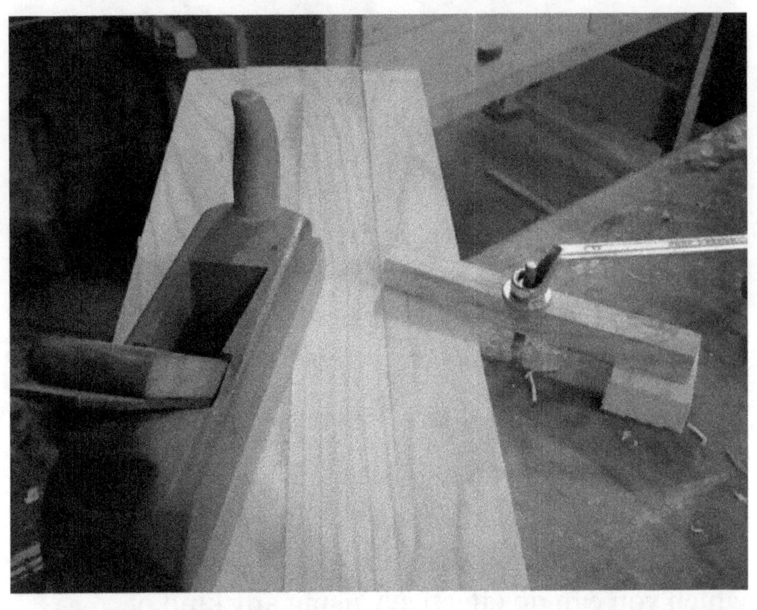

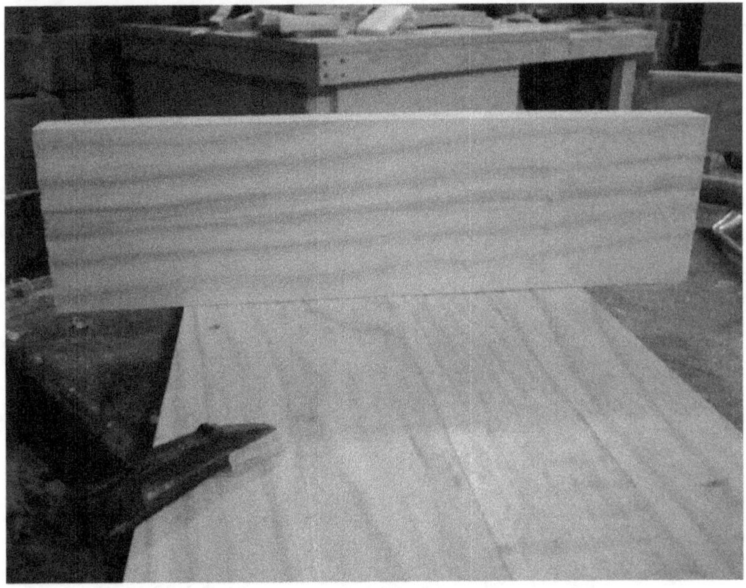

Put a flat piece of wood down and draw a straight line along with that particular flat wood. Remove the wood and stop when you reach the line. Use anything that is available to you to sand it out and repeat it at every end of the board that requires to be flattened. But, don't remove too much wood.

In the same manner, flatten the top and bottom sides of the board as you did to the ends of the board earlier. You can use a hand plane to achieve that and use a piece of straight scrap wood to check whether the sides are flat.

If eventually, you made the mistake of creating a dent in the wood while planing it, use some wood filler to fix it. The next step is to sand the product, which you can do effectively using any kind of sandpaper or hand sander.

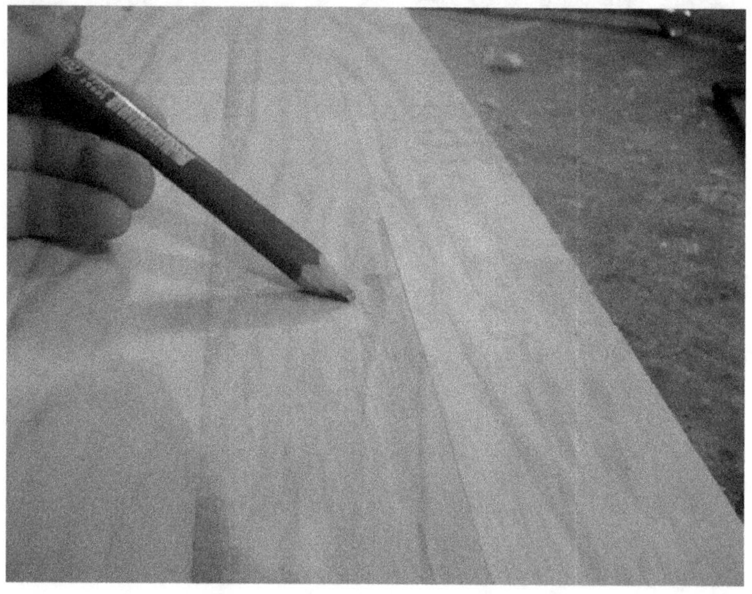

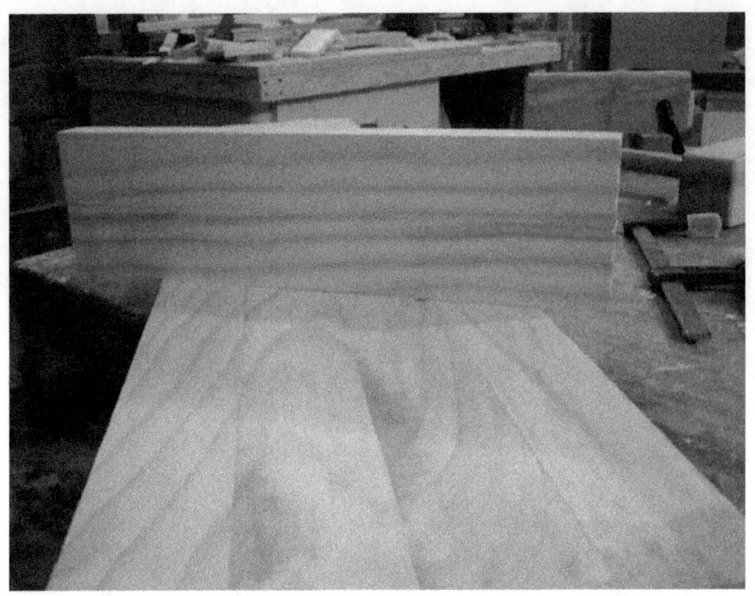

Sandpaper may not save a lot of time, but it produces a better effect. If you're sanding by hand, use either sanding block or some pieces of hardwood between sandpaper and your hand.

Step seven: Cut the wood

Since your board is now flat and rough sanded, it's time to cut it to the pieces needed for the stool. You'll have to cut a total of three pieces, 2 for the leg of the stool and 1 for the top.

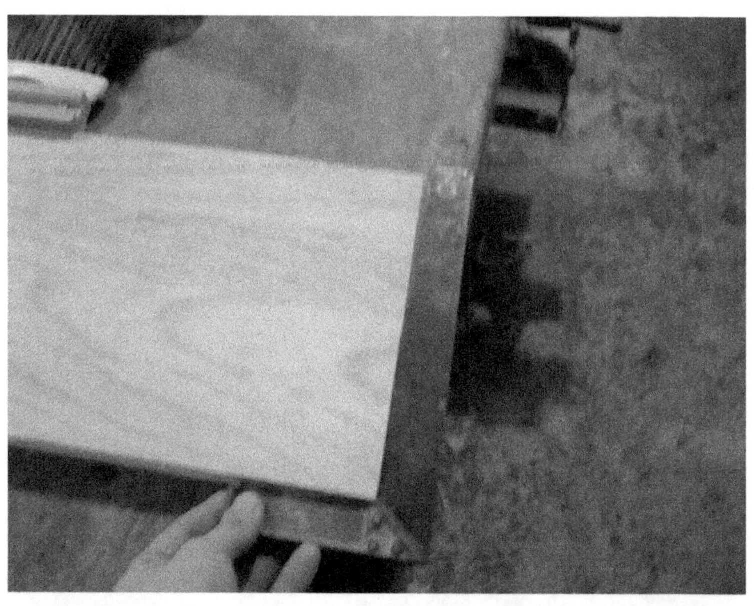

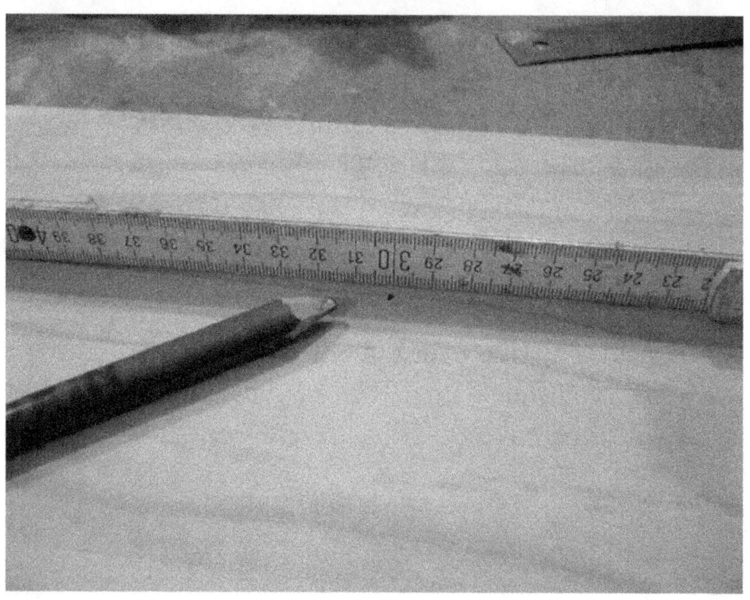

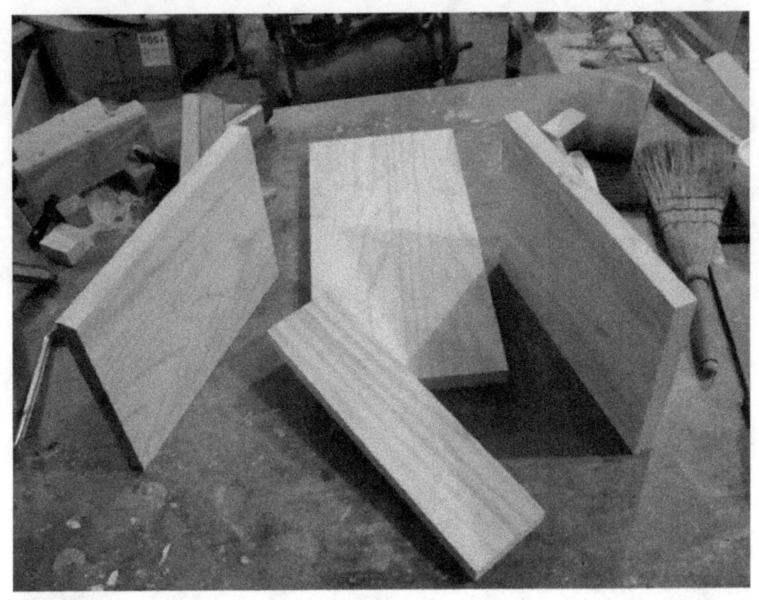

Use a hand saw or any other device for cutting. Cut the board on one side to make a square and remove glued pieces that are unequal finish. Check that it's square and move on with marking. The next step is to mark the legs and top board with 11.8 and 16.5 inches, respectively, then cut through.

Step eight: Draw a layout and create a dado joint

The legs of the stool should not be a block of wood. So, you need to draw a layout for them. Get a caliper or divider or even a round bucket cover and make a circle of any arbitrary size.

Measure out the bottom side of the legs and add markings on both sides. You can use fewer circles for the bottom pattern. Remember, these dimensions are just guides, you're free to use other circle patterns.

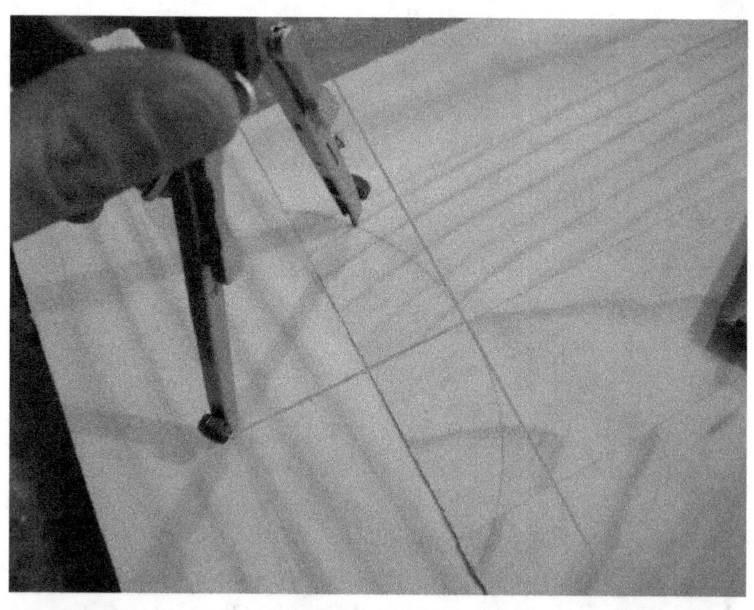

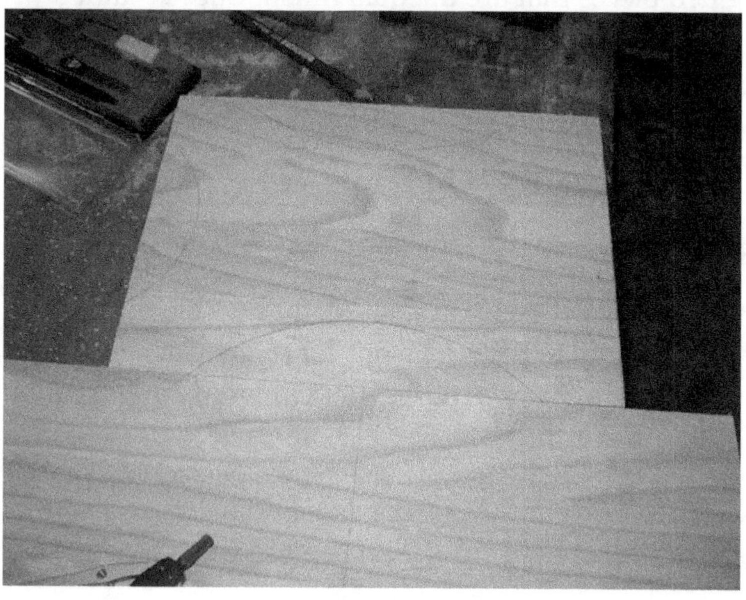

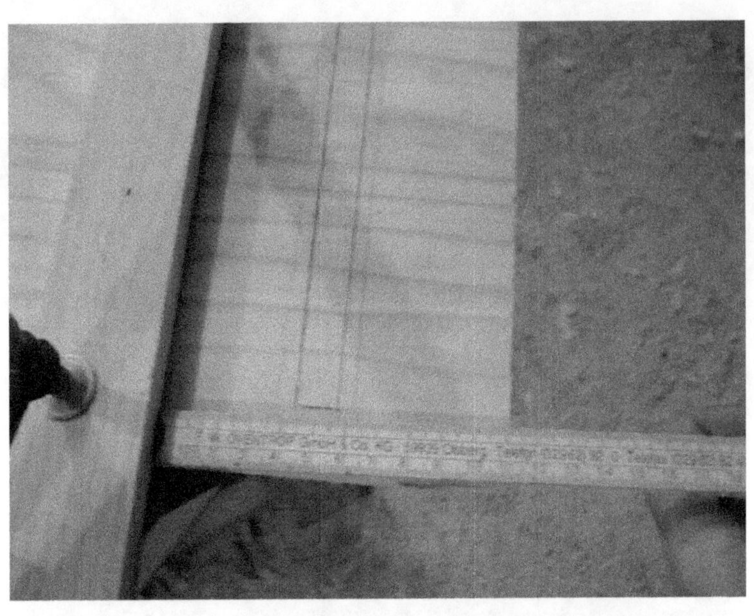

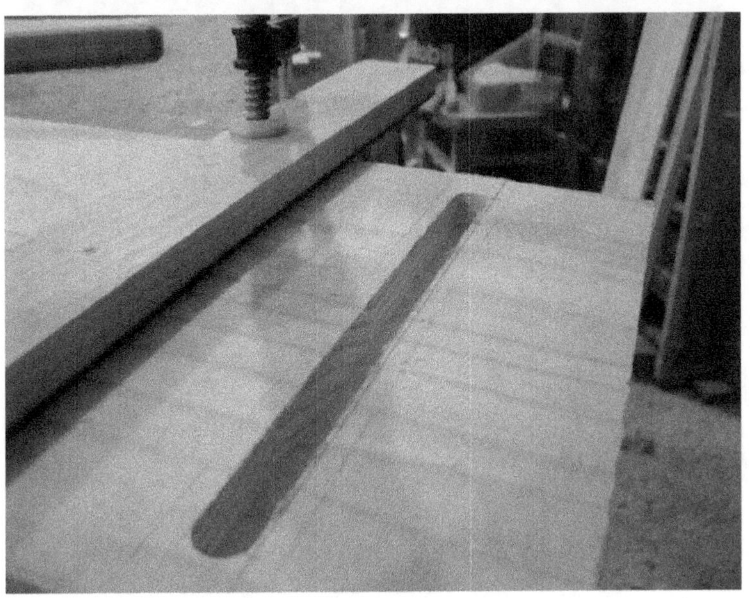

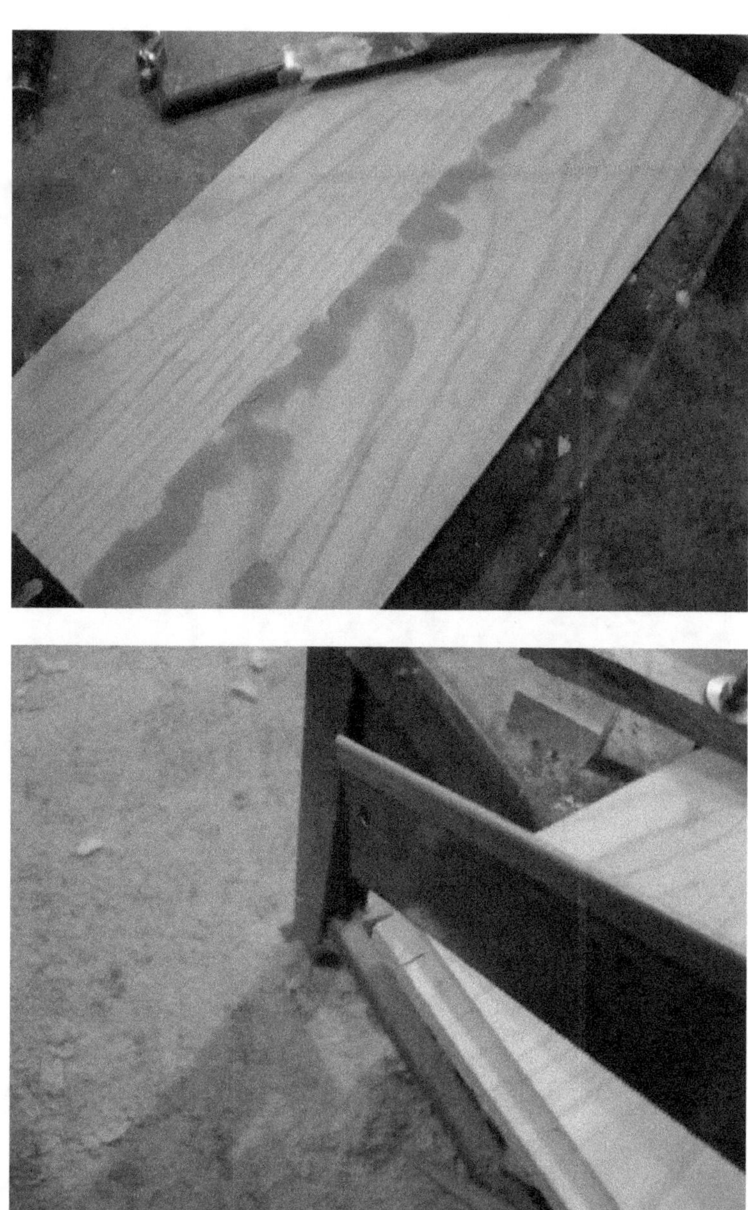

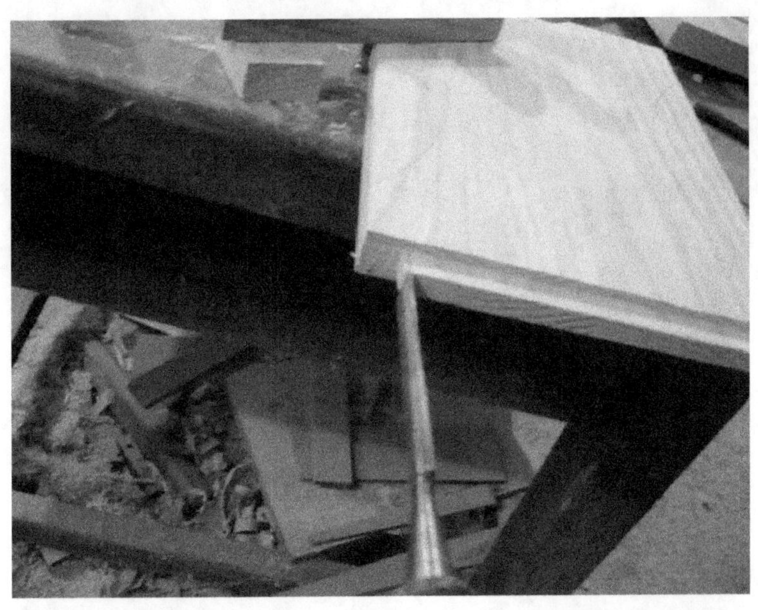

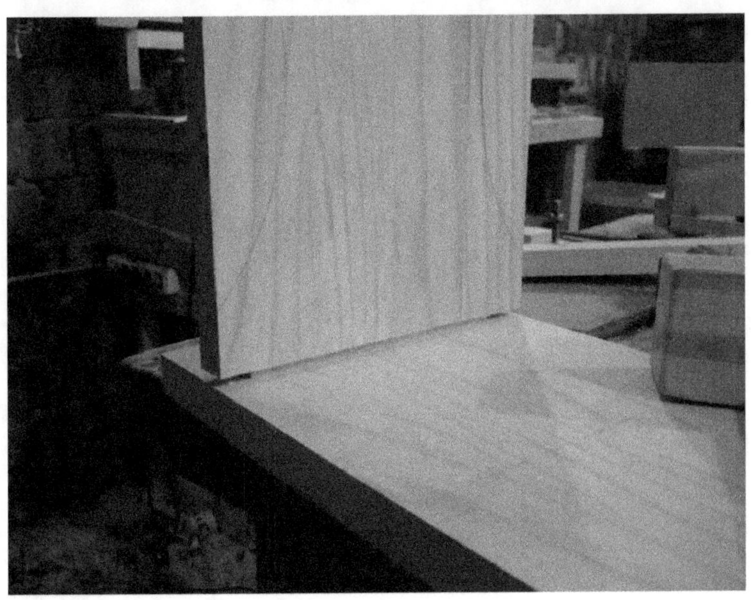

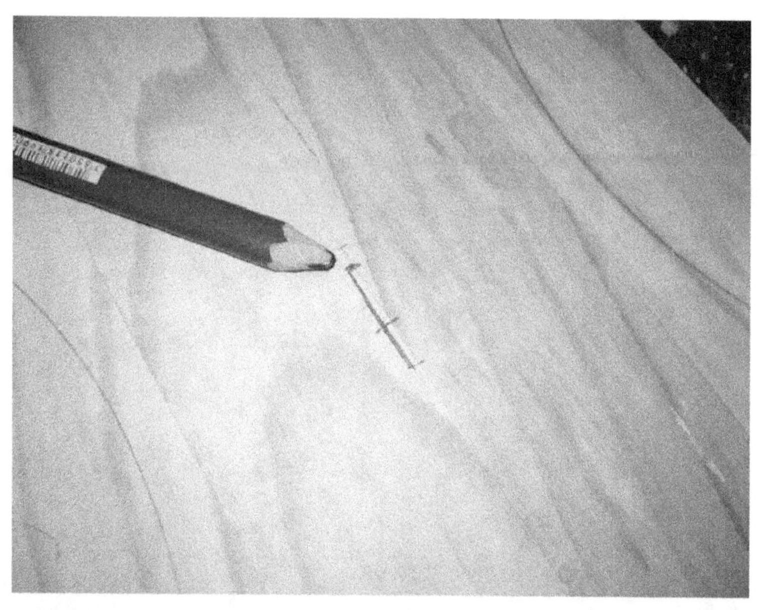

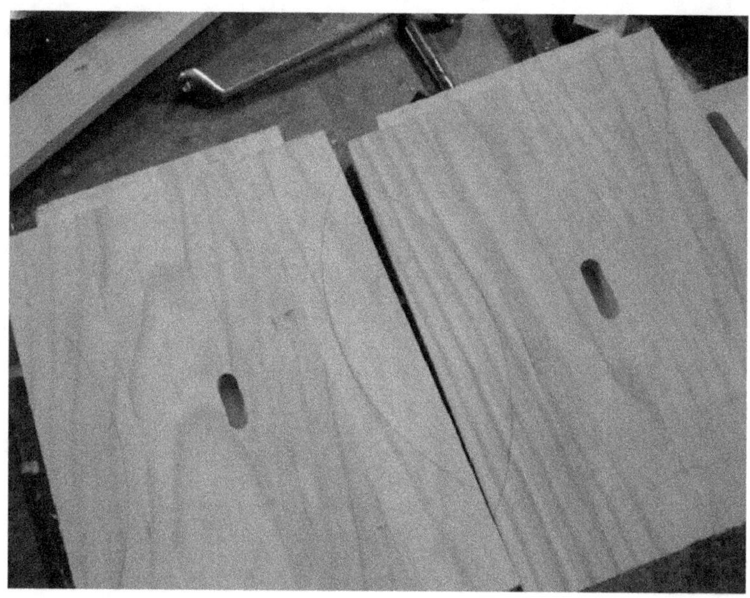

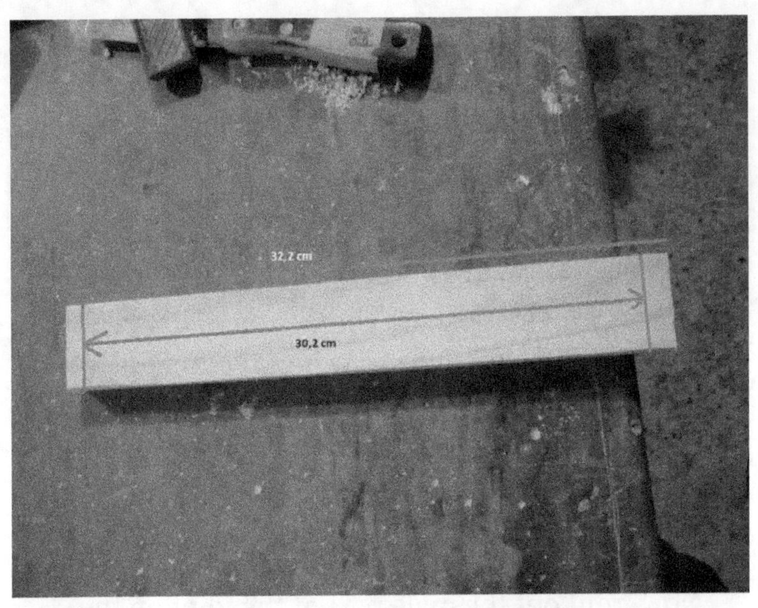

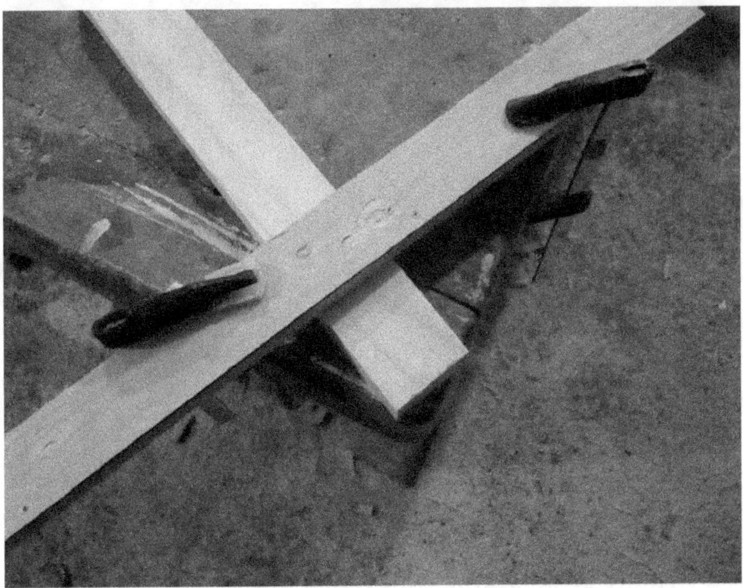

The next step is to make a dado joint. This stage is a bit technical and requires your patience and carefulness. Make a female slot on the bottom side of the top board. Put 2 inches of the legs inside the board and 0.2 inches from the edge of the board.

Look for a router, as it is the best tool at this stage. Use a 0.5-inch straight bit and rout 0.6 inches deep. To rout the female joint, use flat guide wood. After these measurements, mark the distance between the guide wood and the edge of the board and note it. When you want to rout the other side of the board, just put the guide wood at the same distance from the edge of the board. That's all for the female part of the joint.

Now, rout out the male part of the joint on the stool's legs. Make the male parts of the joint 0.55 inches wide and 0.5 inches thick to correspond to the width of the female slot. The male part of the joint is to be made on both legs, as well as on the side that will attach to the top board.

Having determined and made these markings on the wood. Clamp your work very tight using guide wood, just as you did before. Rout the two legs simultaneously and cut 2 centimeters of the male joint from both sides of the legs using a chisel and handsaw. Your joint should fit snugly. But don't join the legs to the board yet.

Prepare the connection piece between the two legs by first of all making female slots of the legs of that piece. Again, dado joints are needed here. You'll need to make slots on the inside of the legs. Locate the center of the leg and mark the slot vertically, making it a little smaller than the connection piece. Use guide wood to rout the slot on the two legs.

Measure the space between both legs to make the male part of the joint on the connection piece. Cut the connection piece slightly bigger for the male slot on each side. Rout the wood to make a male piece of joint, use a hand saw to remove 0.2 inches from the male part of the joint to fit it to the slot.

Step nine: Cut the layout on the legs and sand

Do you remember the markings you made earlier? Now is the time to use them. You can use a hand saw for the cutting. Cut by the line and not into the line. After cutting, sand the surfaces to smooth them using sandpaper for edge sanding.

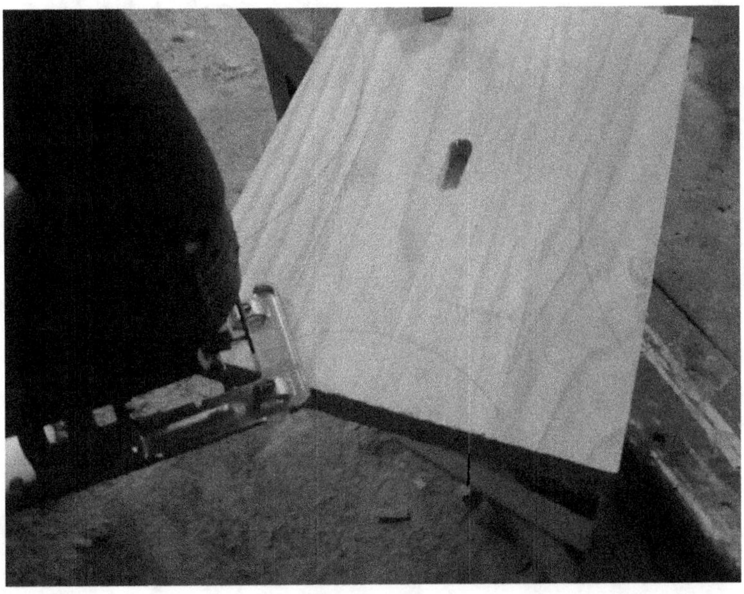

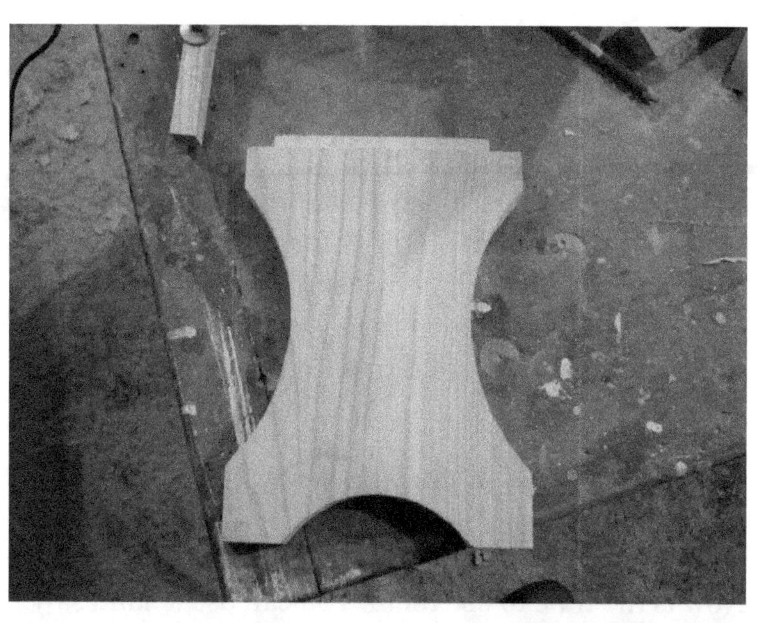

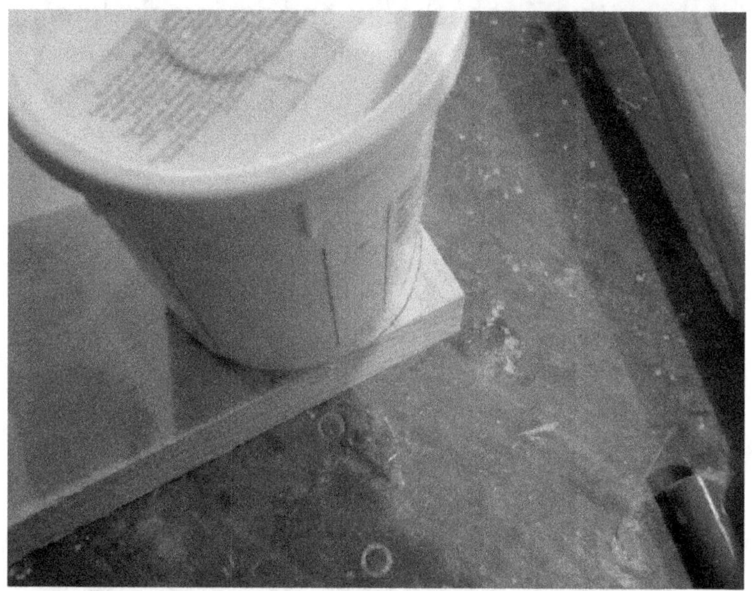

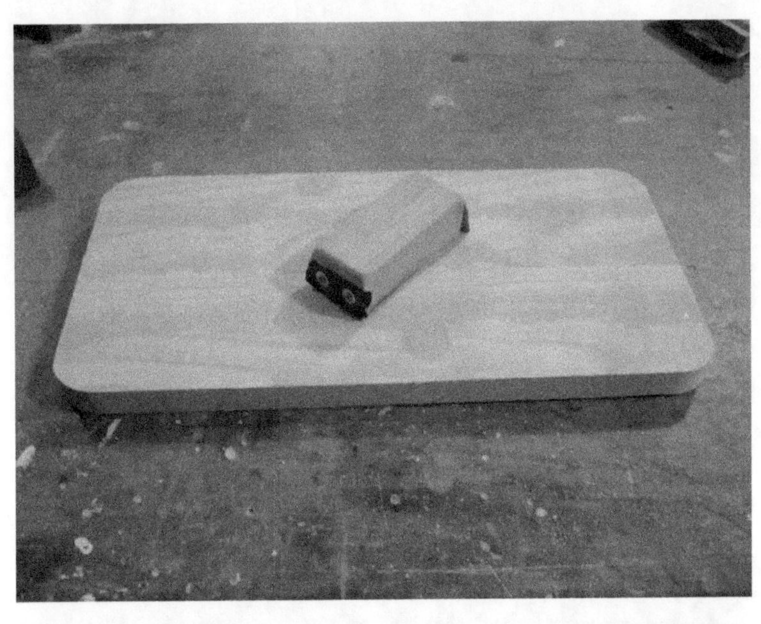

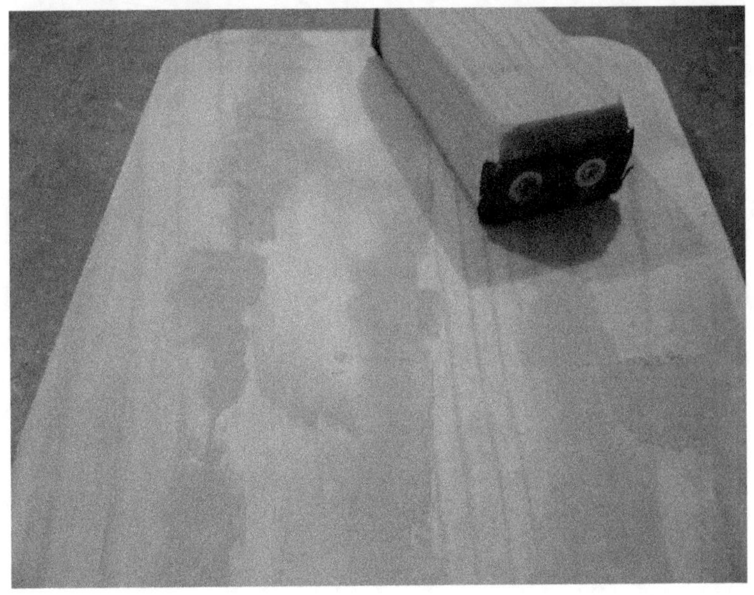

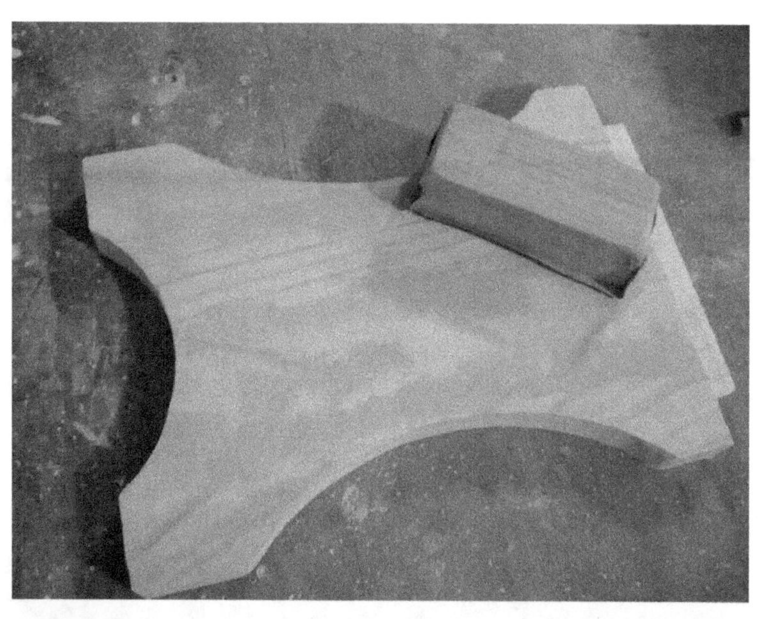

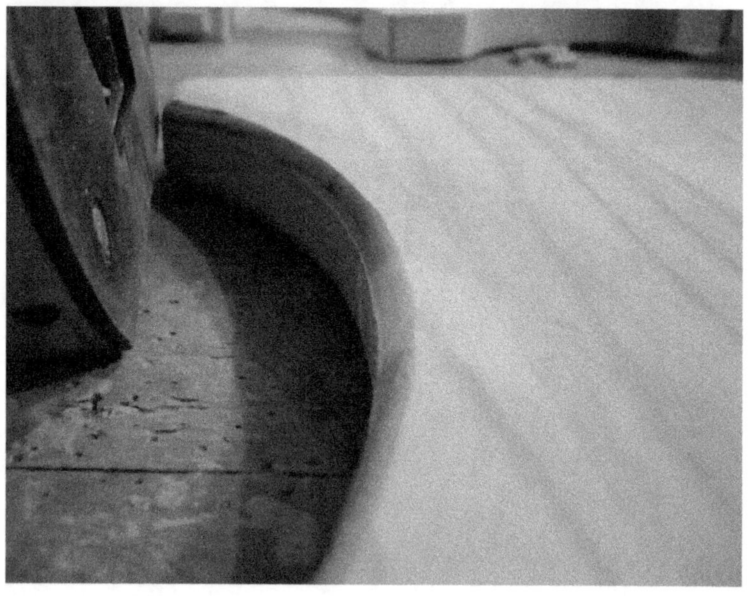

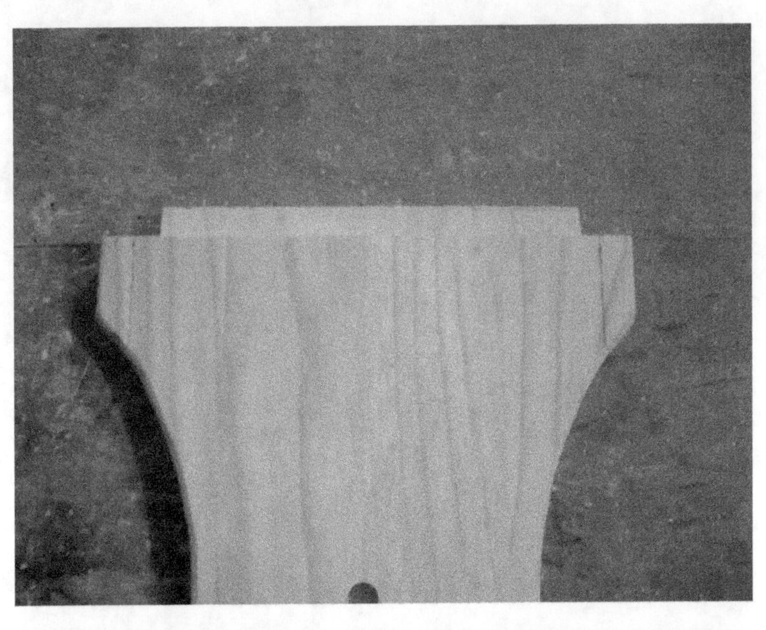

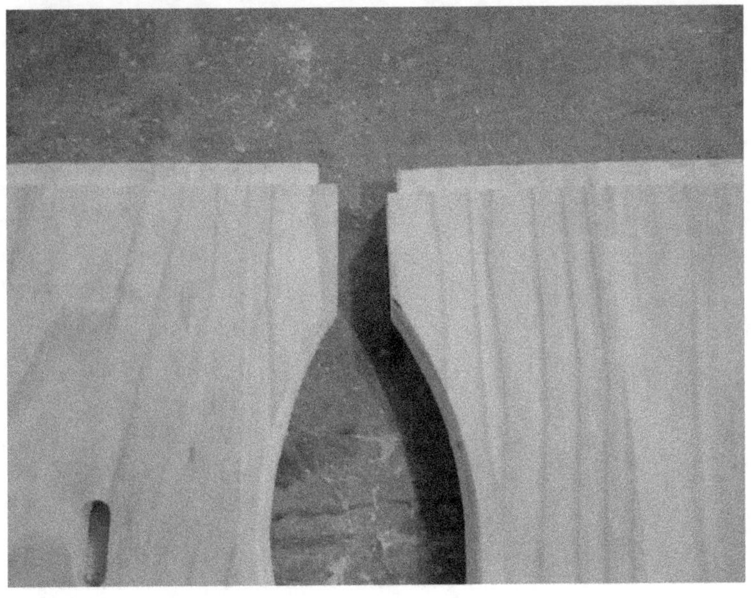

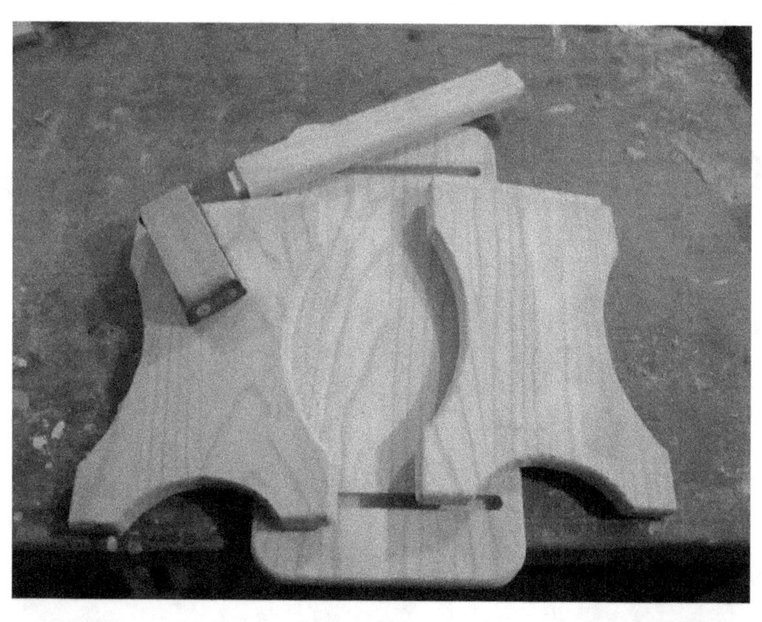

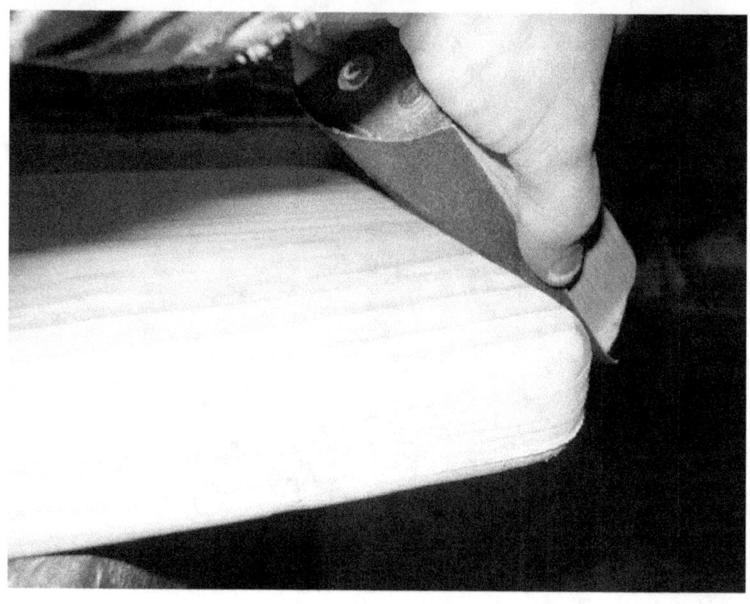

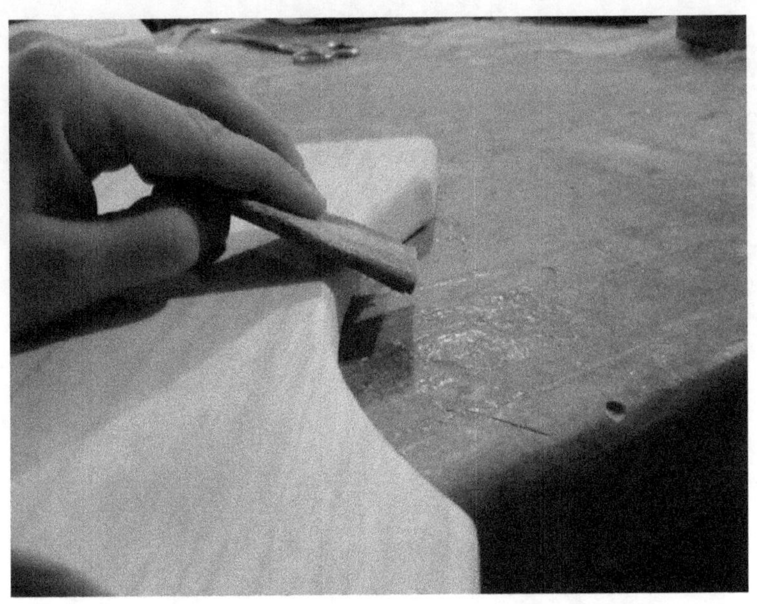

If you curve the stool's leg, apply wood filler where necessary and allow it to dry. Then, sand those surfaces again. You know that a sanding belt is not required here, therefore use a sanding block and a piece of either 120- or 150-grit sandpaper.

Then, fine-tune, or profile, the edges. To profile the parts very well, use a router and round router bit or opt for a file and sandpaper. Just insert the right bit into the router and profile the edges. You may sand the entire parts again to ensure there are no rough surfaces remaining.

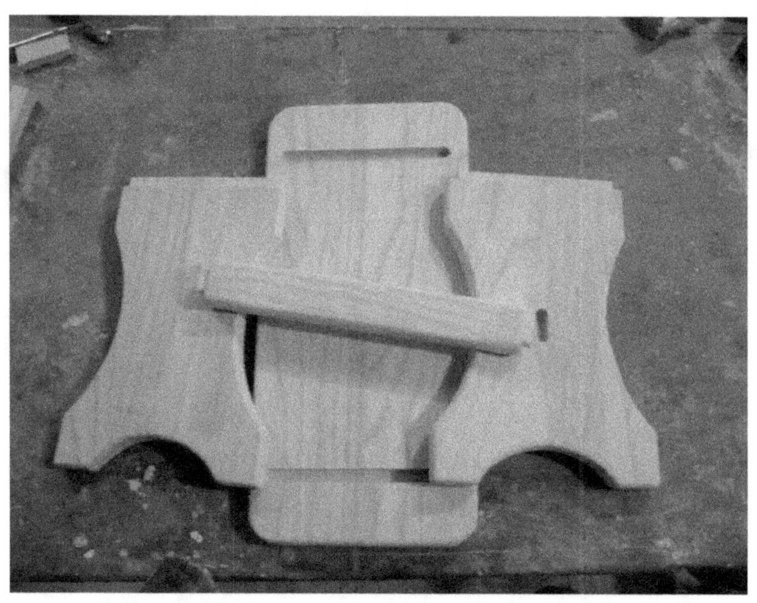

Step 10: Put the piece together

Since you're using dado joints, your joints require to be put together and they'll last for many years. So, kindly put the parts together and use your big mallet to drive them in. You can check whether the legs of the stool are properly aligned and flat. Just place the stool on a very flat surface and if it teeters, check for the leg that is longer and sand it accordingly.

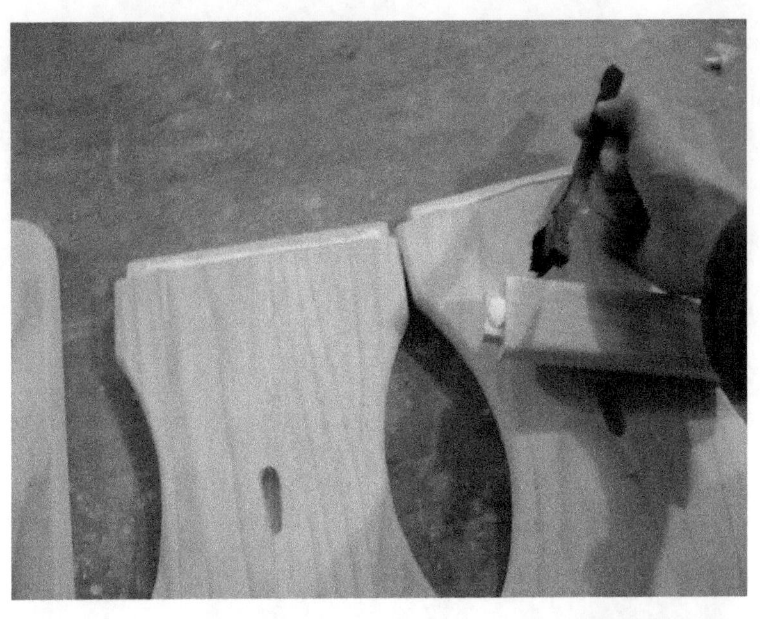

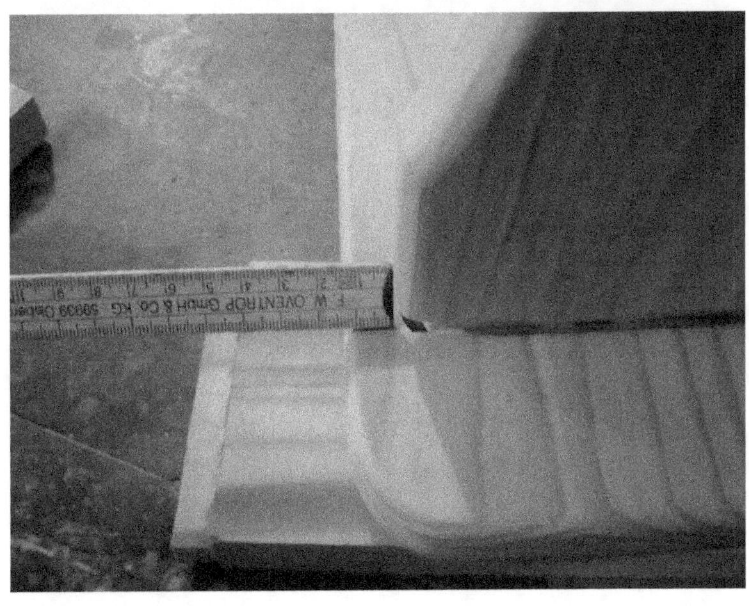

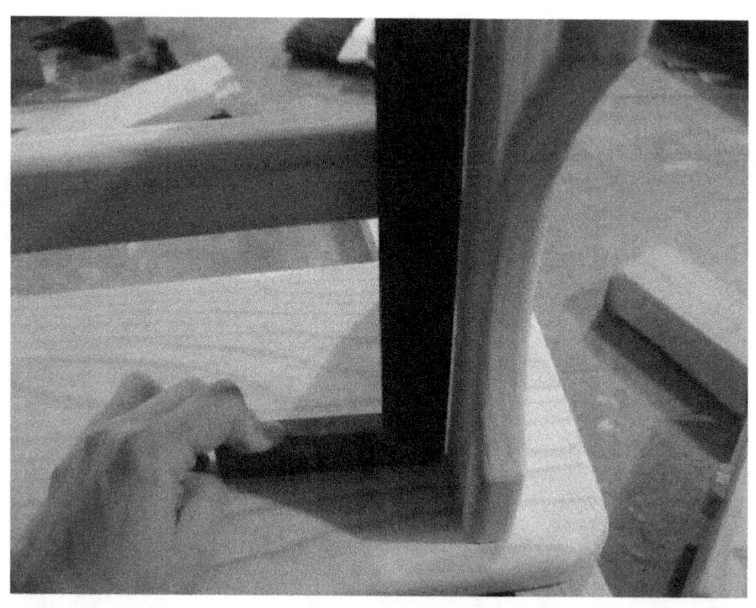

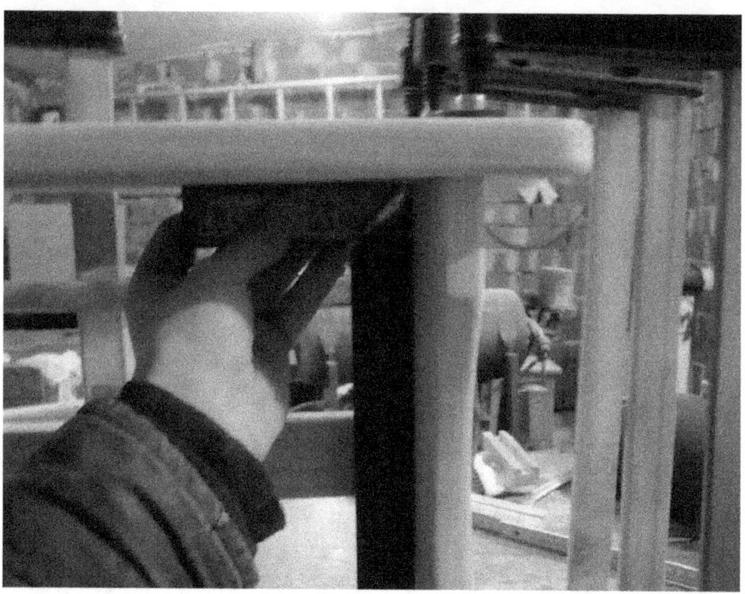

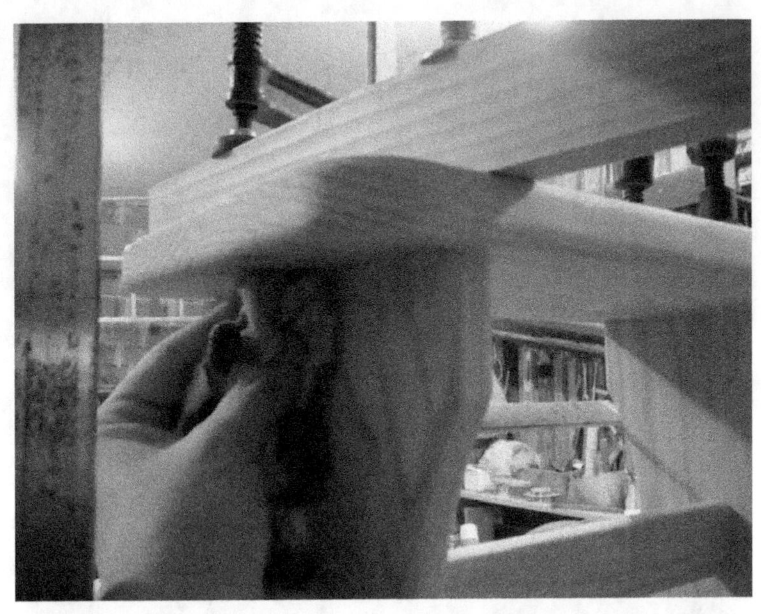

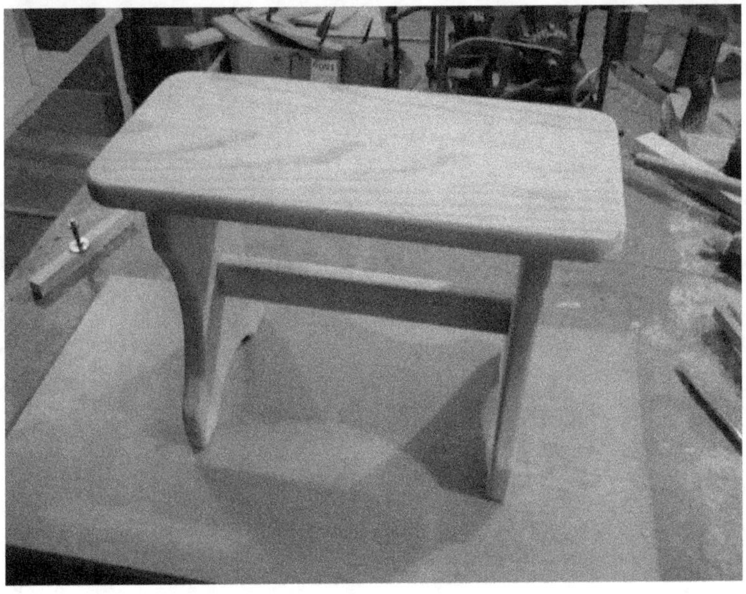

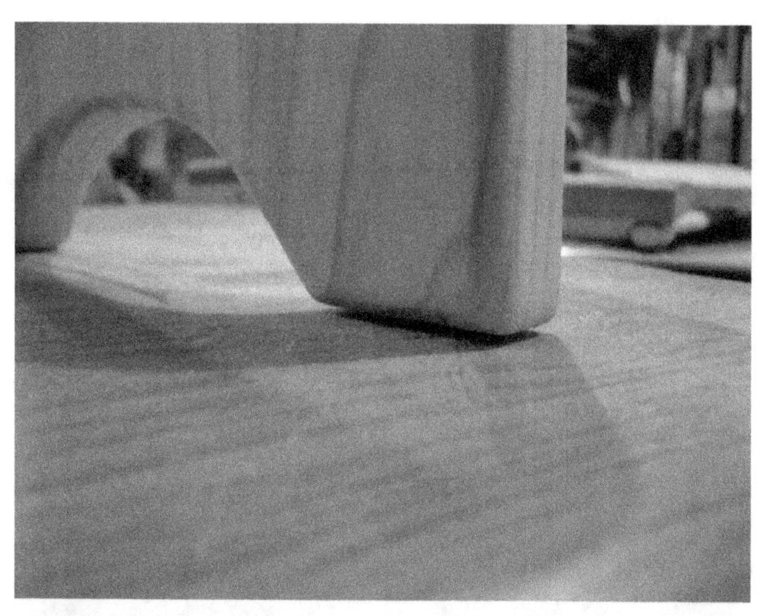

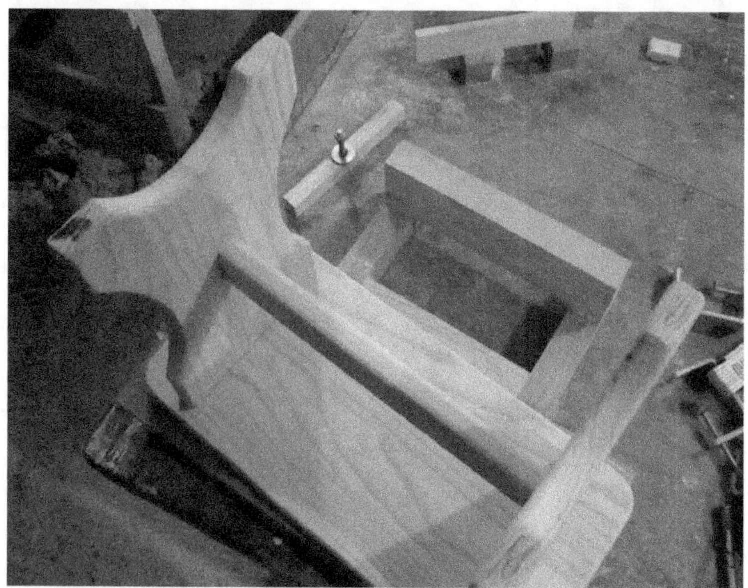

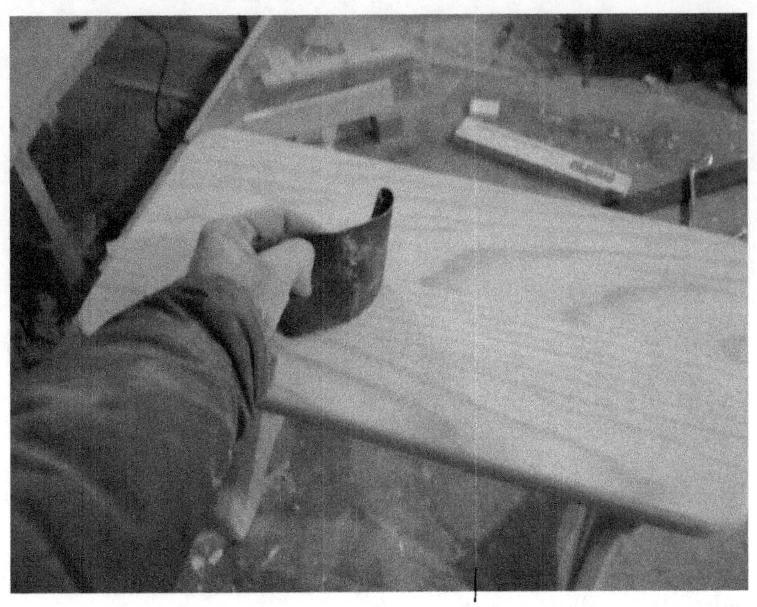

Chapter Summary

Now that you've learned how to make a live wooden object, you can begin to visualize the maximum possibilities of creating an advanced product. In the next chapter, you'll learn about a slightly more complex project of making a tool chest. Come along, as the ride promises to be interesting and enjoyable.

Chapter Seven:
Create A Tool Chest

A tool chest is a great way to keep your tools organized at home or in your workshop.

It is more than just a place you can keep your tools. It's an essential part of your toolset no matter your level of proficiency. In other words, whether it's DIY or a professional car garage, a good tool chest is an absolute need. Bearing all this in mind, you should make every effort to build a tool chest that is strong, reliable, and efficient.

Why Do You Need A Tool Chest?

Here are the reasons a tool chest or toolbox is such an essential thing to have:

- Your tools are in a convenient place, ready for you whenever you need them.

- They're also safely and securely stored away.

- An organized tool chest can make your tasks easier, faste, and more effective.

- Having tools in a box or chest keeps them protected and reduces the risk of damage.

A tool chest, as the name sounds, is similar to a chest of draws. The tool chest is bigger in size and their largest design feature is to store as many tools as needed. You'll typically find tool chests in the home or professional garages. They are stationaries, although some may have wheels to enable easy transportation. Their size and weight are not the best design if you regularly need to take your tools from job to job.

So, how do you make one based on your knowledge of Japanese carpentry and joinery? Well, that's very simple. Here are the steps to follow.

Step one: Choose the right dimension and cut the wood

Deciding whether you want your tool chest to be big, small, or of average size is the basic step to follow. Of course, your choice depends on the number of tools you would want your box to carry. Generally speaking, you want it to house even your longest tool—the saw.

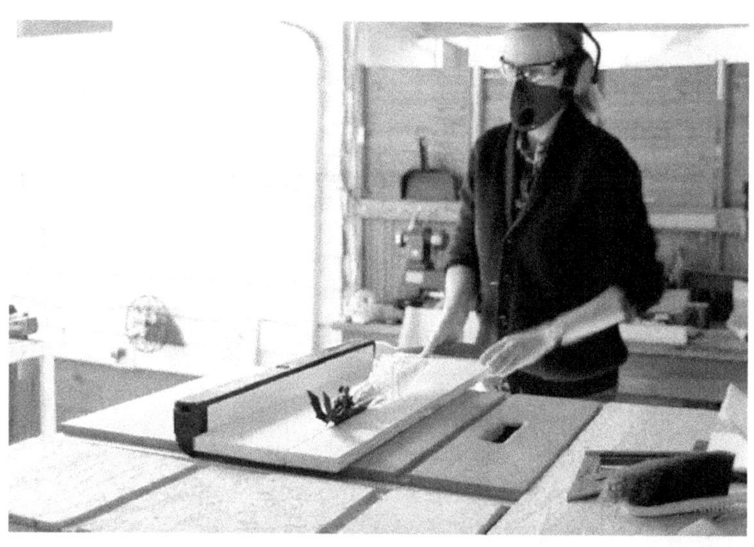

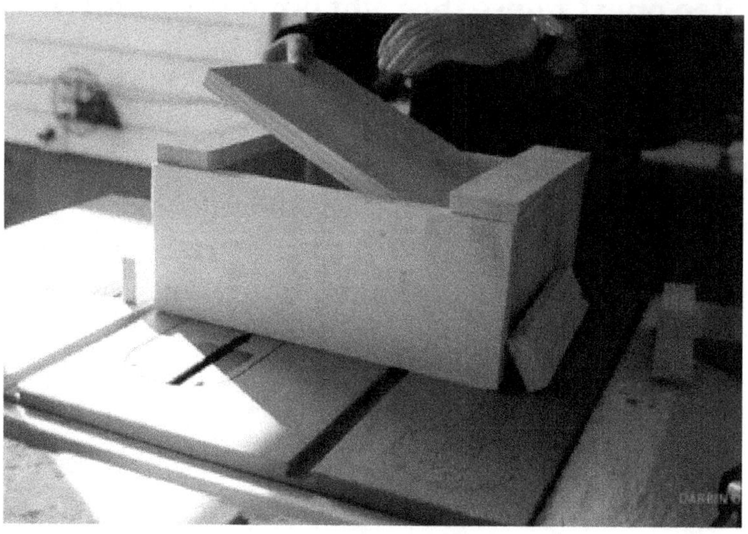

For this project, use 1x10-inch pine wood and cut the pieces to size. Use the following dimensions:

A. *1 @ 15 x 9.25 inches (bottom)*

B. *2 @ 15 x 6 inches (long sides)*

C. *2 @ 9.25 x 5.25 inches (short sides)*

D. *2 @ 10.75 x 2.5 inches (top sides)*

E. *1 @ 10.75 x 1.5 inches (lid side)*

F. *1 @ 10.75 x 2.5 inches (wedge & wedge fitting, cut in the middle at an angle)*

G. *1 @ 9.25 x 11 inches (lid)*

H. *2 @ 2 x 9.25 inches (handles)*

I. *2 @ 4.5 X 2.25 inches (feet)*

Step two: Get the handles and wedge ready

Simply cut a curve for the handles using the hand saw and chisel. In the same vein, you should use the hand saw and chisel to cut the wedge at an angle. See the pictures below:

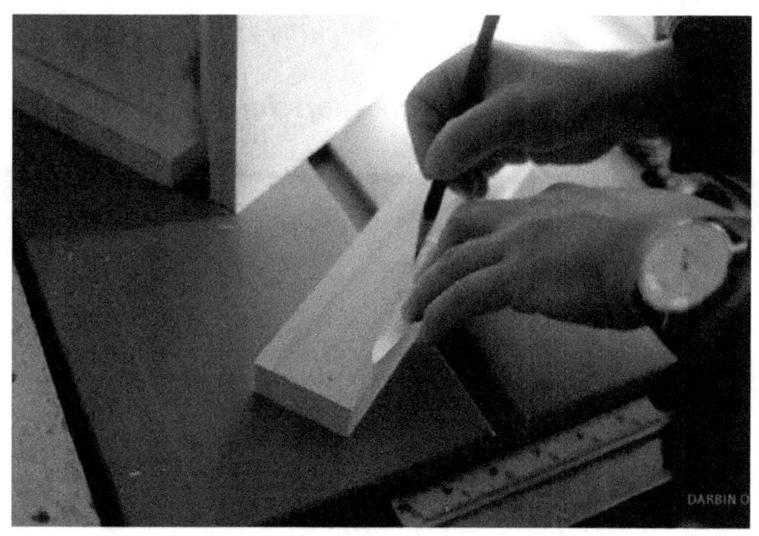

Step three: Prepare the hand tools

The hand plane can assist you in cleaning up the angled wedge while the spokeshave does the work of smoothing out the inside of the handles.

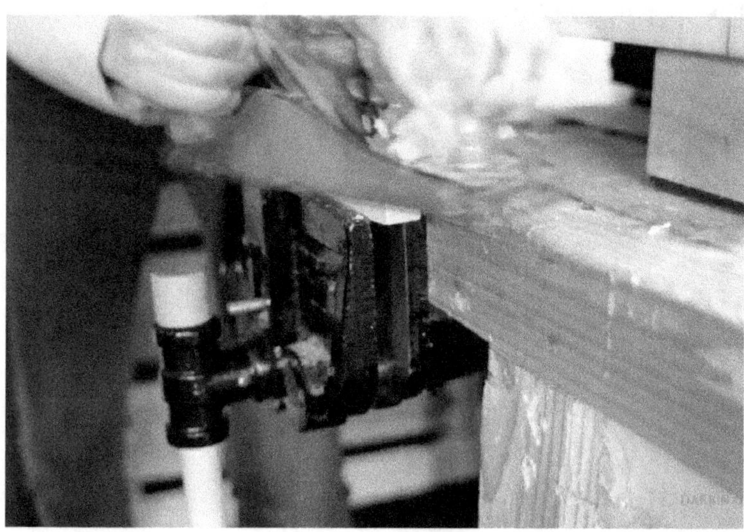

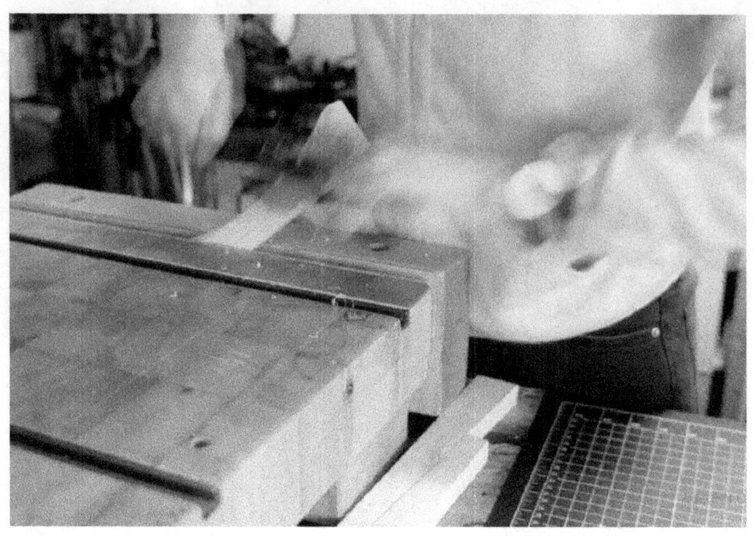

Step four: Mark and create holes

At this point, you need to mark out the spots where all the plug holes would go to hold the box firmly tight. After marking these spots, begin to create these holes. These holes are necessary as they add to the beauty of the box and make it strong, eventually.

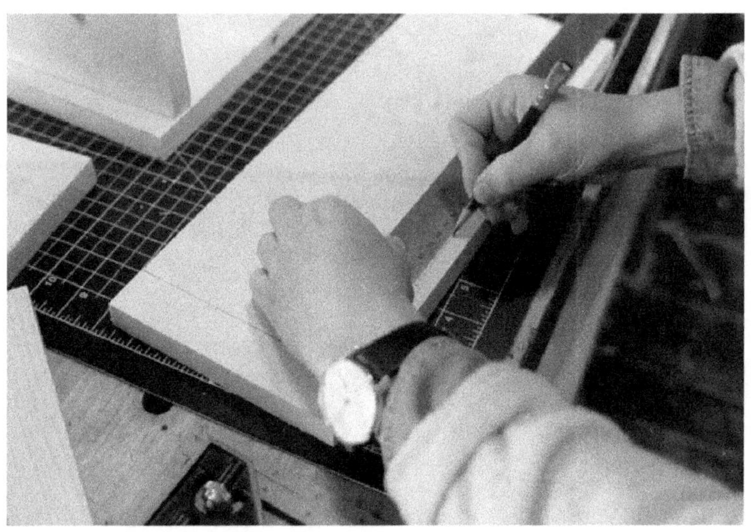

Step five: Assemble the parts together

Once the holes are drilled, it's time to assemble the pieces together with the help of screws. Traditionally, the method of joining Japanese tool chest is through wooden plugs as they are easier to use and they offer the opportunity for plugs to work well.

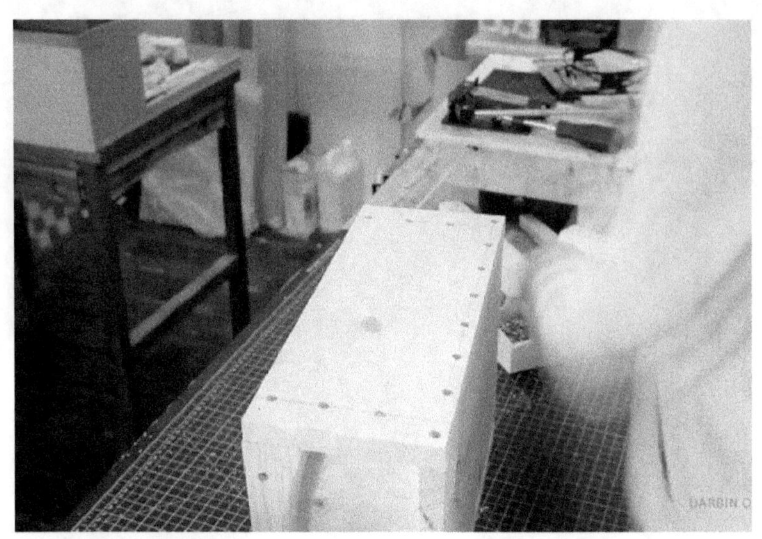

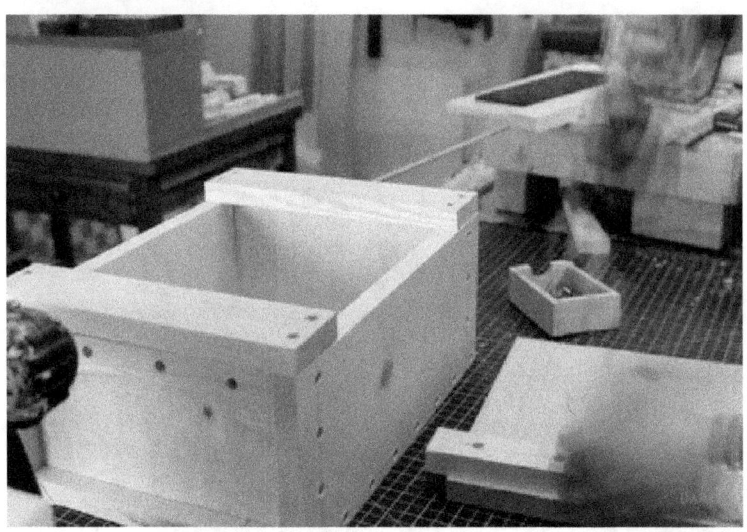

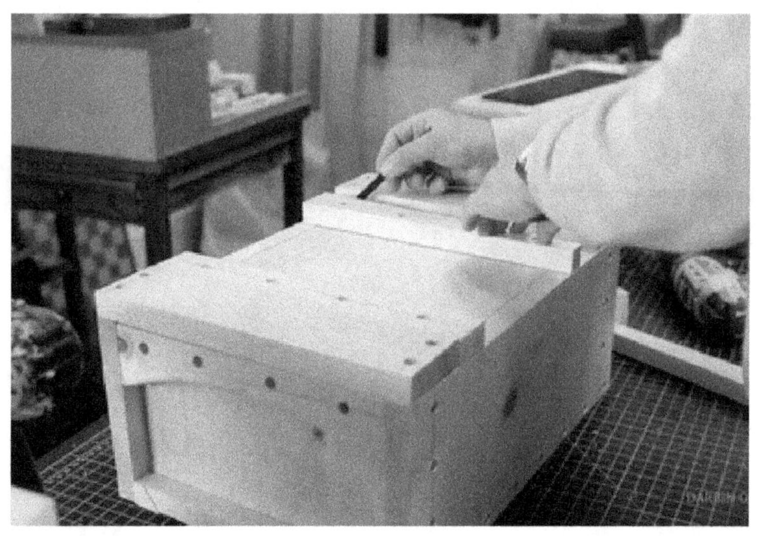

Step Six: Add legs to the base

If you wish to slightly bring the tool chest up from the ground, then you can add about 0.25 inches to the product.

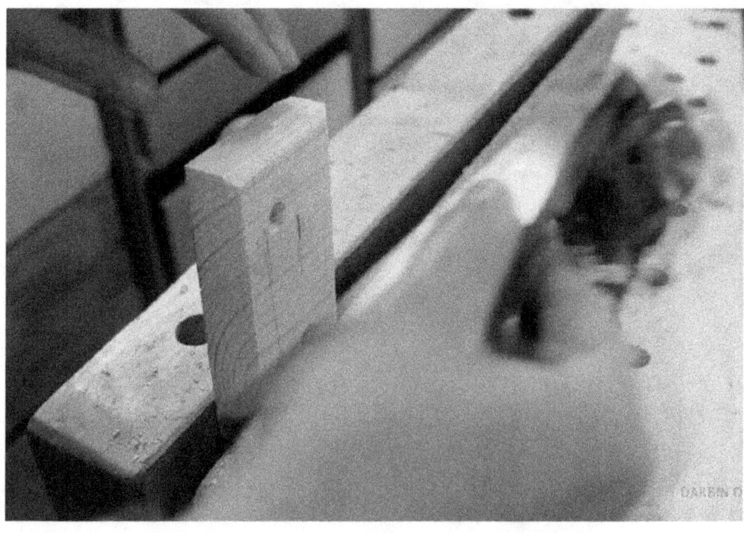

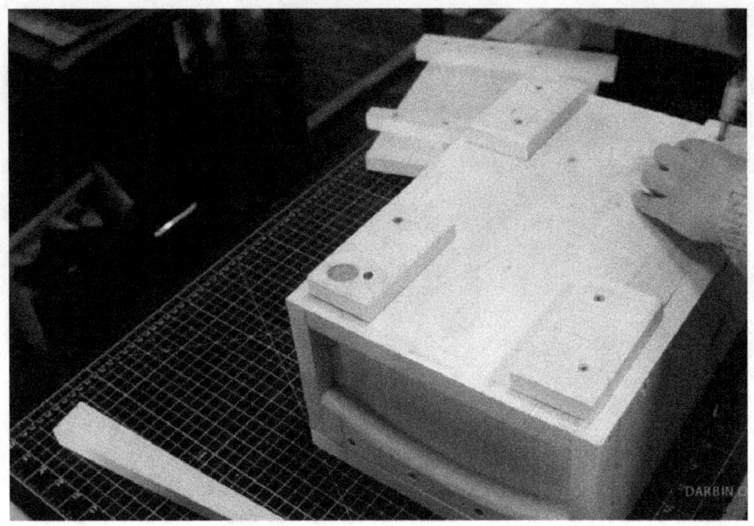

However, this step is an optional one. You can ignore it or implement it, if you want to.

Step seven: Create a space for the handle

To make the tool chest very easy to carry and lift the cover whenever the need arises, you will have to drill two holes in the cover (lid). These holes should be large enough for some rope to fit in and pass through.

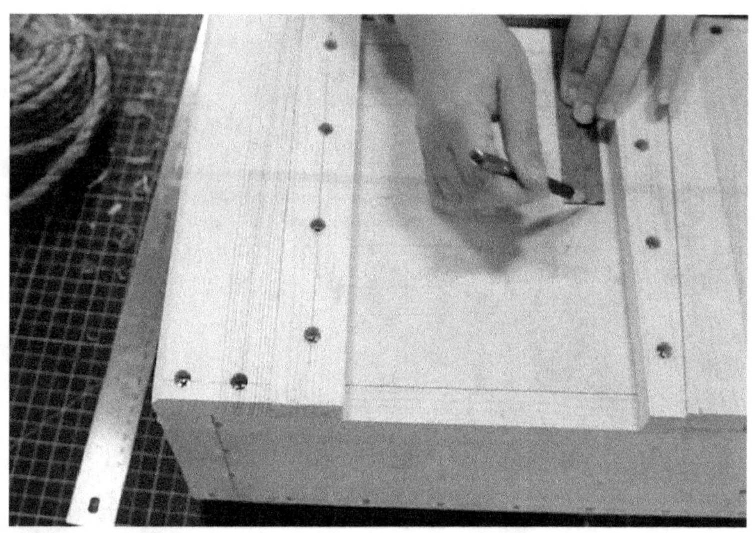

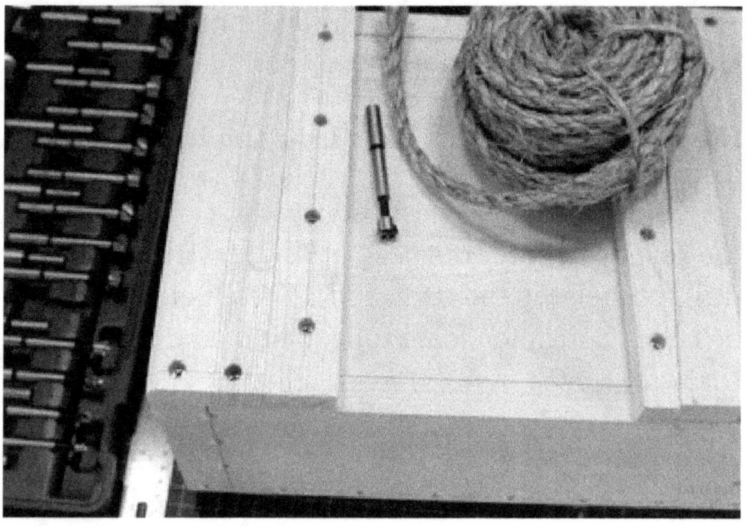

Step eight: Sand the box

Now, you need to sand every part of the box to make it look nice, smooth and beautiful. Just use your sandpaper to obtain uniform sanding of all the surfaces.

Step nine: Stain the tool chest

This is yet another optional step. You may decide to either stain some parts or the whole box, or you may wish to leave it natural, the way it is. The choice is yours.

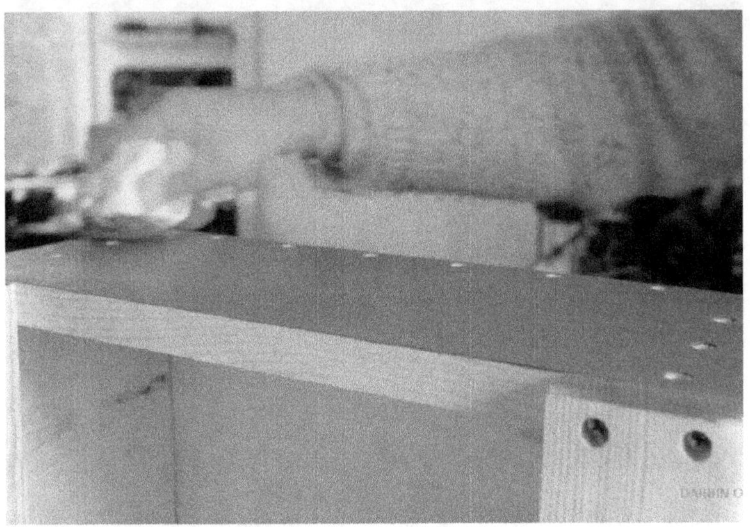

Step 10: Insert the plugs

At this point in time, you need to fill in the holes with screws. So, measure the depth of the countersink. Then, set up a stop block on the bandsaw to cut the required plugs. Apply a bead of glue on each plug and use a mallet to securely push them inside the holes.

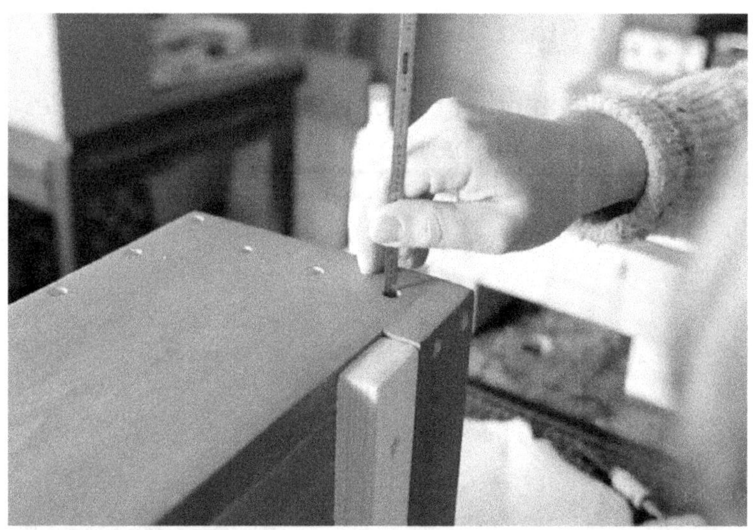

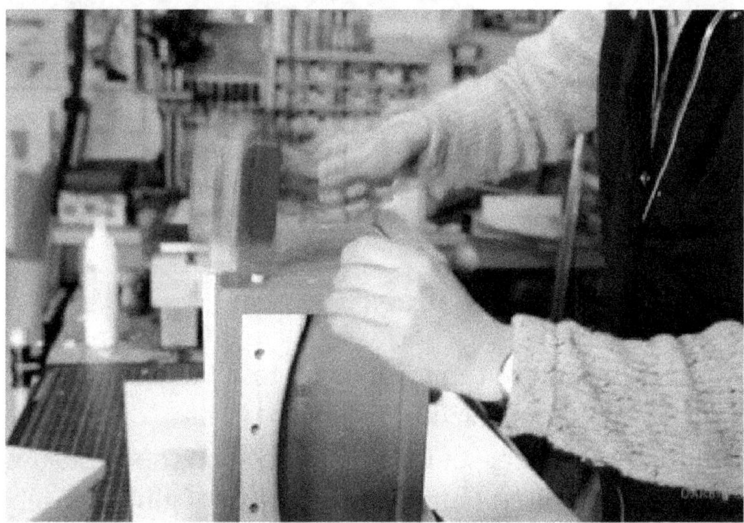

Step 11: Sand those spots

To make the inserted plugs look nice, neatand smooth, call your local sanding machine (sandpaper) back to work. Use the sandpaper to sand all the spots where you inserted the plugs to make them smooth.

You can even apply stain to those areas if you wish to make them look uniform.

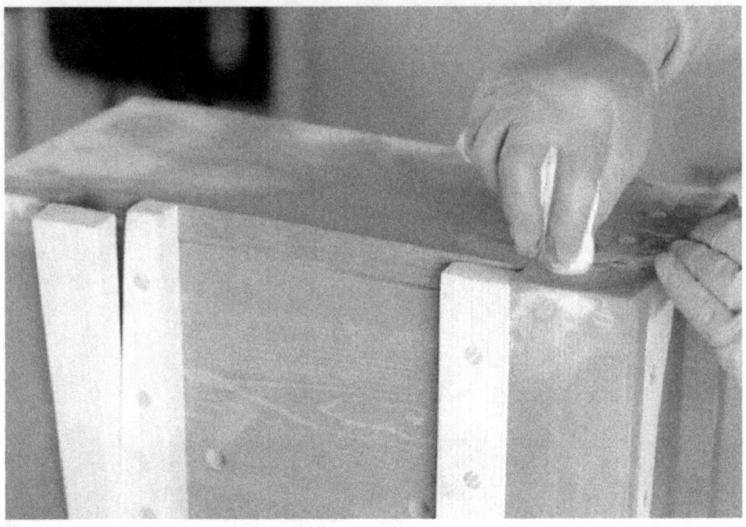

Step 12: Fix the rope

At this last step, you have to add the rope for the handle. All you'll have to do is to simply tie two knots on the underside of the cover (lid) to securely keep the handle in place.

For a final finish on the box, you may decide to put a touch of shellac all over the outside of the box to beautify the chest and give it some protection.

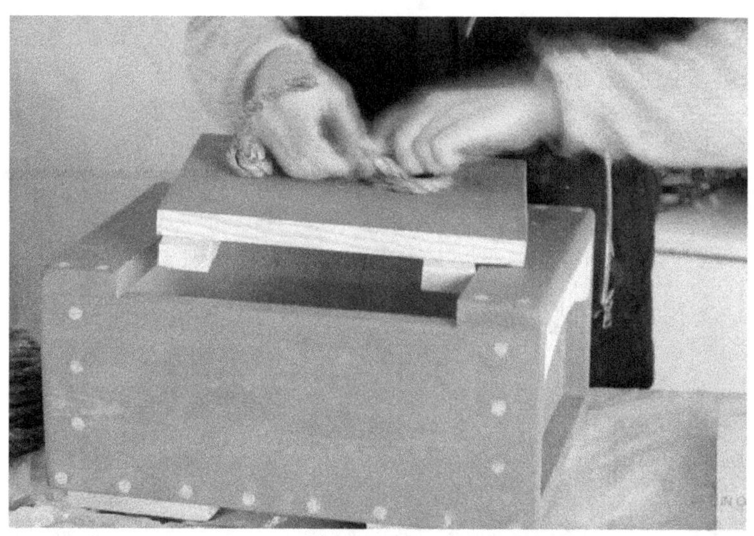

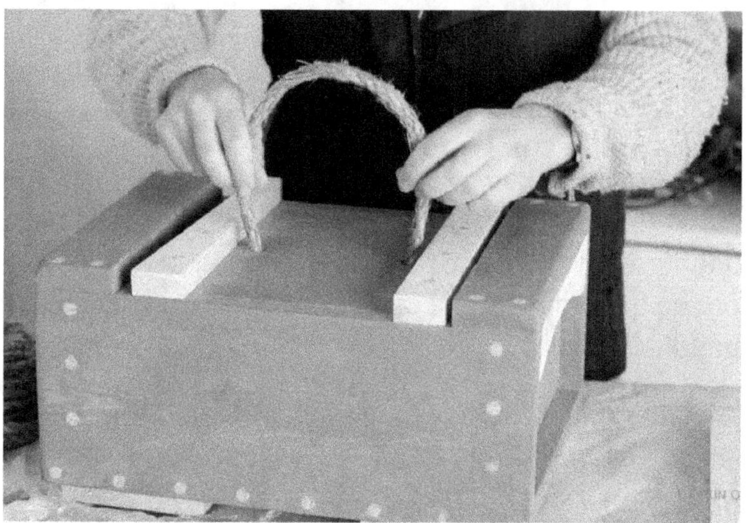

That's all for this classic Japanese tool chest.

Chapter Summary

The above project was an interesting one, in the sense that it took us to the practical class of building a tool chest from scratch using the Japanese joinery concept. With this tool chest, your tools will now have a place to stay for easy location. If your tools are organized, your work will be organized, too. This project is pivotal to your success as a craftsman.

Chapter Eight:
Make a Dynamic and Beautiful Dinner Table

You've tested your hands on small projects and become familiar with Japanese joinery. The skills gained from these several projects will make it easier for you to handle tools and other materials. Based on this, you can equally handle large projects. It's now time to create a bigger project—a beautiful dining table.

By the way, how should a dining table be, with regards to space, size and accommodation?

Your first step in choosing the perfect dining table is to consider the space of the room in which it will go. Is the space for a formal dining room the place you use to host dinner parties? Or, will the room be used for everyday settings for homework and most meals? For an everyday-use arrangement, a dining table that is low maintenance but the high style may be your best bet. Make sure that whatever you decide on, you're leaving enough space around the table to comfortably walk around the room and get in and out of the seats.

Understanding the size and material you're looking for may be the most difficult part. From a traditional setting to a more modern style, your dining table can do more or less as you want it to. Therefore, you need to keep it classic with an all-wood option. You can even get loud and select something that will set the pace for style in your dining room. Combined with the most suitable chairs, your dining table should display your lifestyle at its best.

The shape of the table plays an important role in creating an elegant and comfortable space. Presented below is a guide to help you determine what size of dining table you may need once you've chosen the right shape.

Size	Oval & Rectangular	Round & Square
48 inches	4 persons	4 persons
60 inches	6 persons	6 persons
72 inches	6 persons	6 persons
96 inches	8 persons	Not a typical size
120 inches	10 persons	Not a typical size

Understand the fact that every person requires about 24 inches of eating space. Besides, your table should be at least 36 inches wide to give enough room for food and place settings.

Construction of a traditional Japanese dining table

To get started, two beams are secured to the tabletop with sliding dovetails. The legs are set and fixed into that beam with mortise-and-tenon joints. There is neither an apron nor a brace between the legs. As such, there's no leg-to-tabletop linkage. Here is the working procedure for this table. First start with the tabletop, work on the sliding dovetail beam, and conclude with the legs.

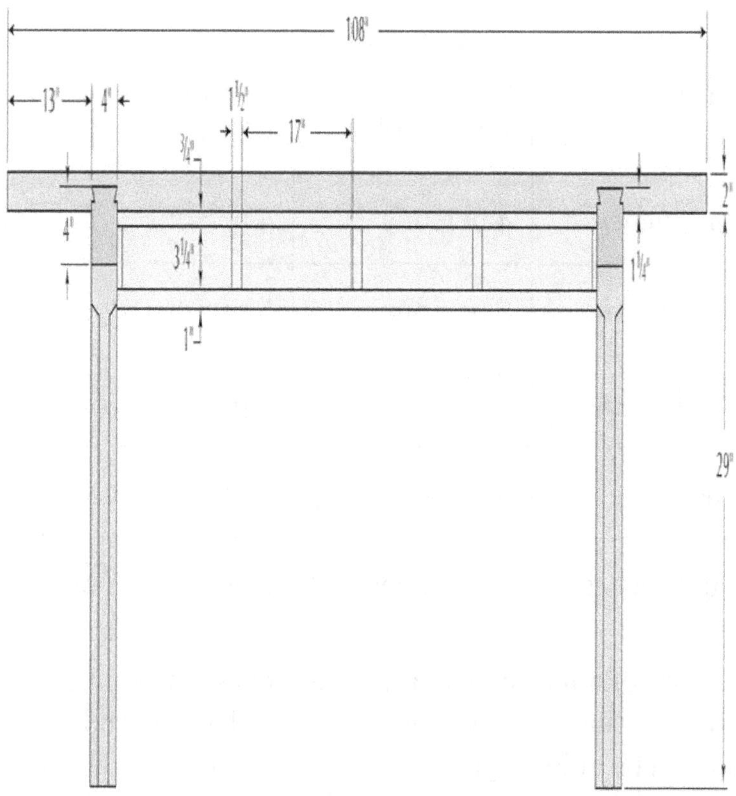

Sketch and Design of the Table

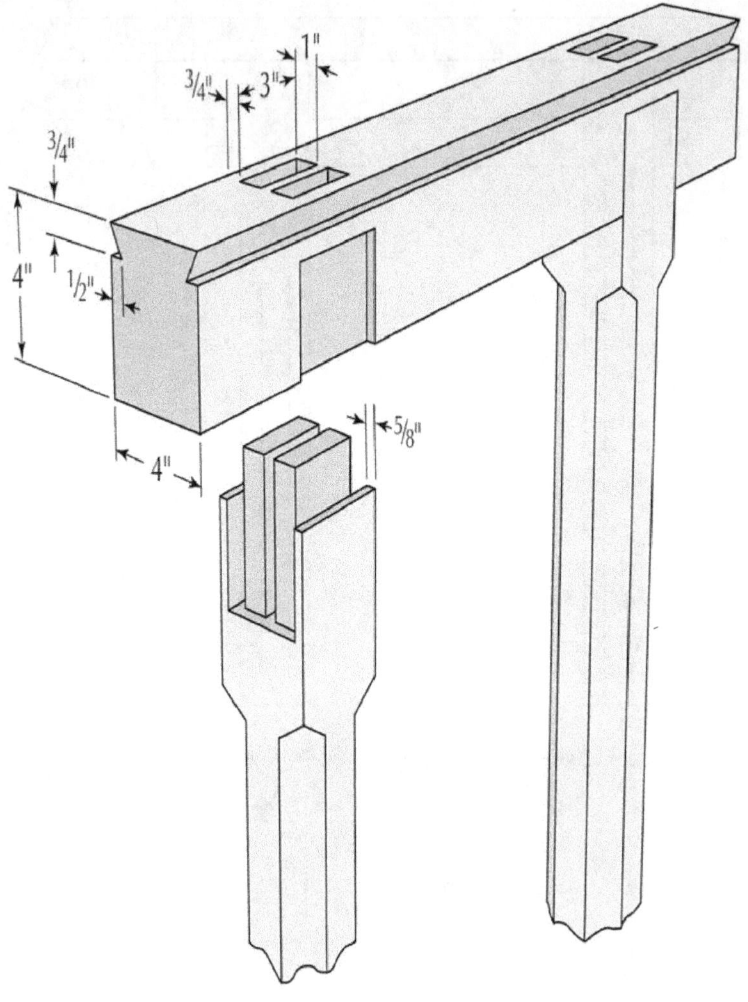

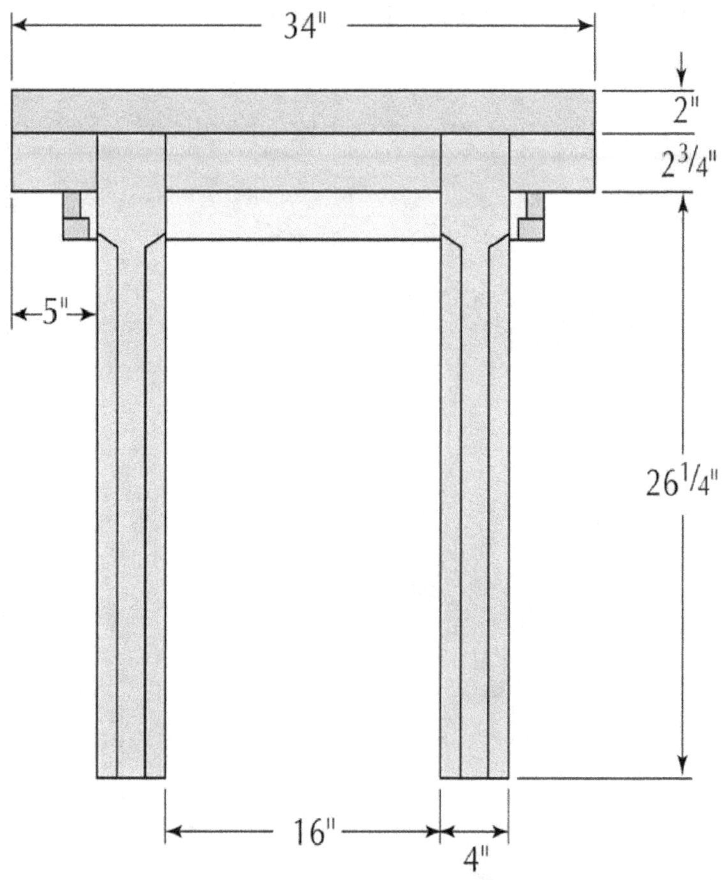

Profile

Dimensions:

Item	Number	Sizes (inches)		
		Thickness	Length	Width
Tabletop	1	2	108	34
Legs	4	4	36	4
Beams	2	4	36	4

Joints that'll make the construction feasible

You need to mark the position of the legs of the table. So, mark the edge of the table all around the beams and decide on the position of the legs. Since the table does not have an apron or leg brace, it means that all the stress retires to this point. You need to design a joint that'll absorb all the stress coming from all angles.

Use double mortise-and-tenon joints and place a non-shouldered tenon on both ends to be in a small space with the tenon joints. The non-shouldered tenon is on the same level as the beam. This ensures that the table is secure in both length and width.

You can achieve this by pounding the beams out and marking the mortise positions. Roughly excavate the waste from the two sides. Then, clean the mortises from the two sides using a Japanese chisel.

You'll need to cut out about 0.63 inches for the non-shouldered tenons that offer additional support to the legs and remove the material to have a smooth surface.

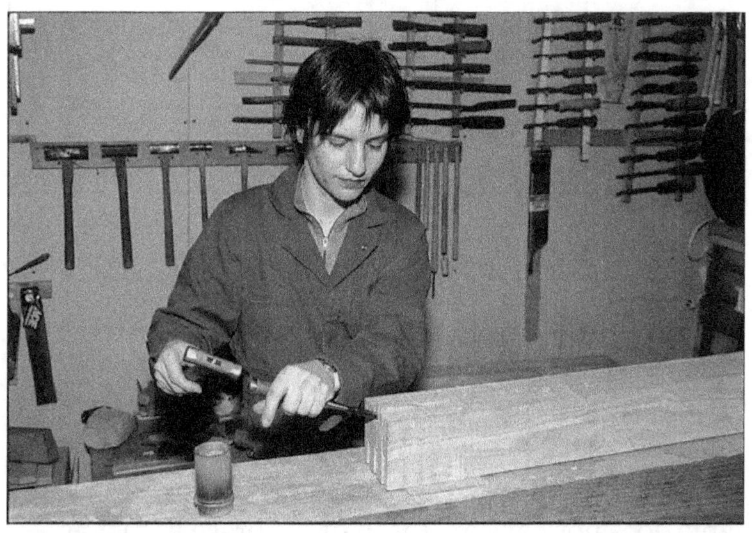

Here are the steps:

Step one: Gather all your wood pieces

You need to figure out how much wood you need for this project and go pick it up. Maybe you have a log of wood (ash) you acquired over the years that has been lying idle in your workshop; this is the time to use it. Or, you can look for straight boards you can find and use. All of the wood needed for this project won't cost you much, less than $100 or thereabout.

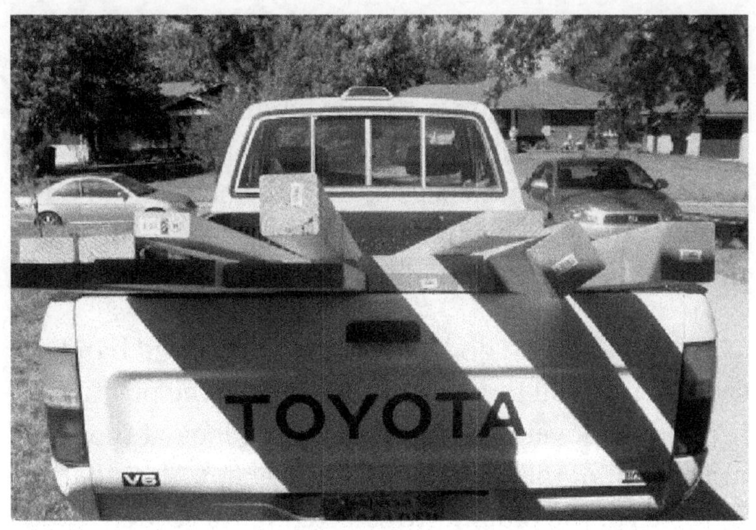

Step two: Cut the wood

It's possible to get the guys at the hardware shop to do the cutting for you, but the ideal thing is to cut the pieces yourself. Mark out the dimensions and cut using a hand saw. Make sure you label each piece of wood you cut so that you don't get confused later.

Step three: Plane the tabletop

At this stage, you have to flatten the two sides of the tabletop using sandpaper. This will carefully remove twist and warp and also keep the top at an optimum thickness. Remember to plane across the grain of the wood.

Also, you can conveniently use 250-grit sandpaper to smoothen the surface of the tabletop.

Step four: Set up the dovetail beam

The dovetail beam is the next item on the list. Considering the fact that the tabletop is about 2 inches thick, then the legs and beam should be about 4" x 4" x 36", taking into account the part of the beam that enters into the tabletop with a tail.

All you have to do is to use the jointer and band saw to create all the pieces. Then, mark the position of the sliding dovetail beams by taking a look at the movement of the wood's grain and color. Also, the four legs of the table were selected in this order — the left and right first, followed by the front and backside.

Go to the bottom side of the tabletop and mark the centerline from one end to the other end with an ink line. Mark the table ends squarely on the two sides of the table from the centerline. The positions of the sliding dovetail beam are marked from the end lines.

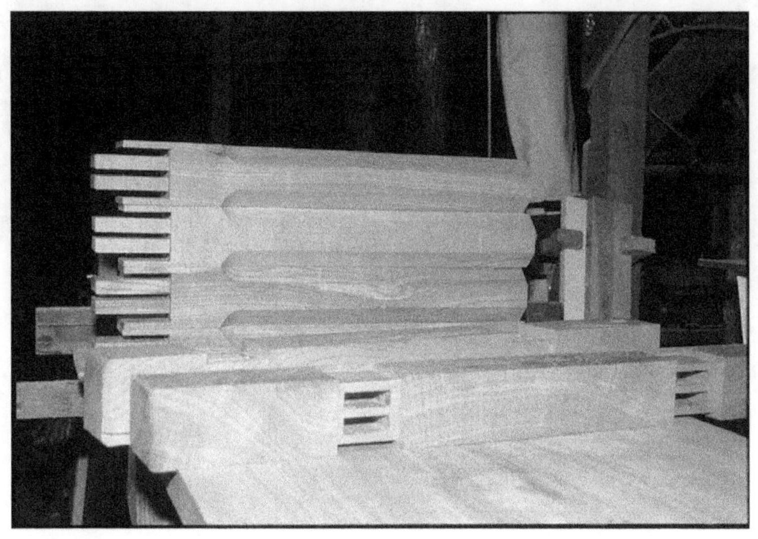

Step five: Create a strong connection

Considering the weight of the table, the design has no connection for its legs and apron under the table. So, depending on just the tail to make the legs strong is not ideal. The best option is to sink part of the beam into the tabletop, together with its tail. This will provide more than enough strength in the brace.

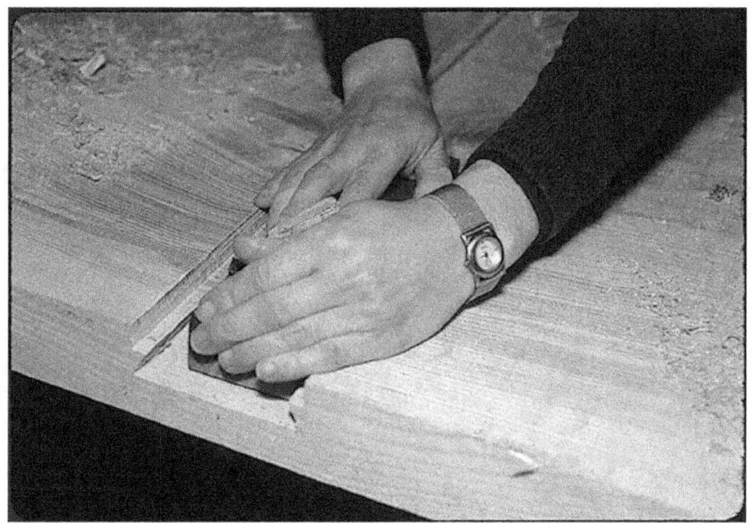

It is important you consider the size and depth of the tail support, as well as decide on the tail's angle before marking out the lines. You can use a narrow Japanese plane, circular saw and chisels to remove the waste. Use a straight edge to check the flatness so as to create the tapered sliding dovetail groove.

Step six: Measure the beam's tapered sliding dovetail

With a knife and marking gauge, mark the beam's tapered sliding dovetail, and use the table saw to roughly cut out the tail.

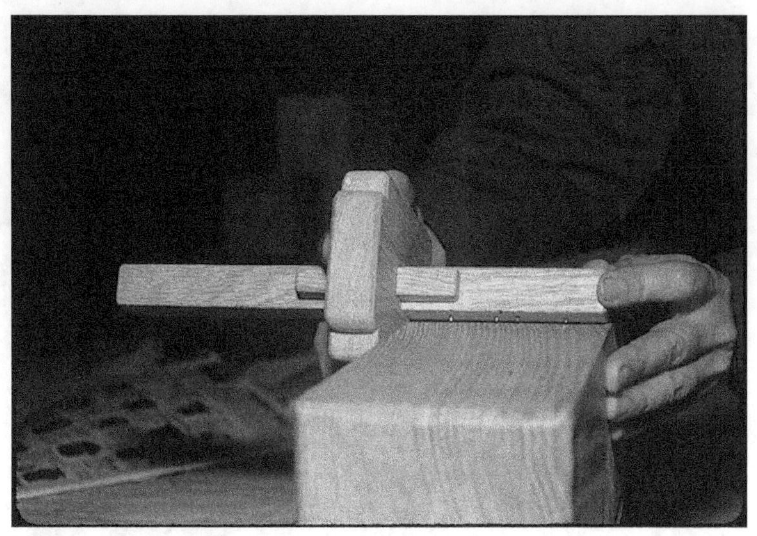

Carefully plane both tails using a planer and chisel. Test the fit while you work. Finish the pins and tails of the joint and cut a large chamfer on the two ends of the tail beam. Then, pound the beam into the groove using a big mallet.

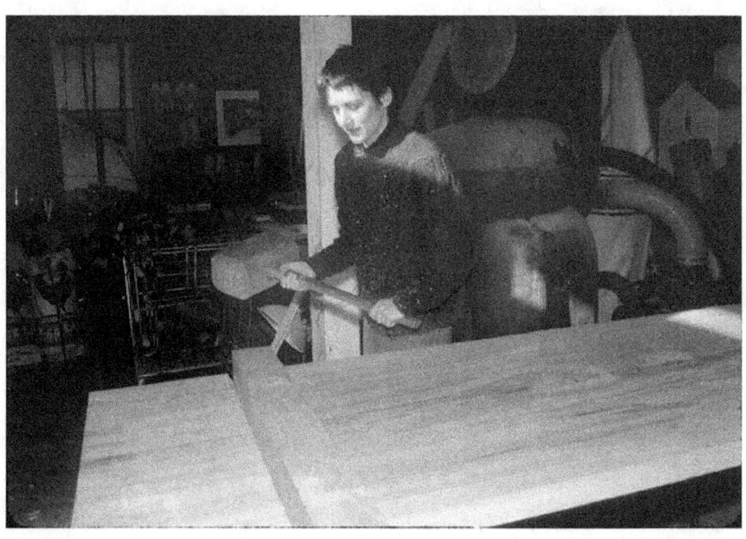

Step seven: Cut the ends of the legs

Test your skills here by cutting the ends of the legs cleanly and squarely. Mark the tenons and rip the leg's tenon with a Japanese handheld ripsaw. Use a chisel to remove the materials in between.

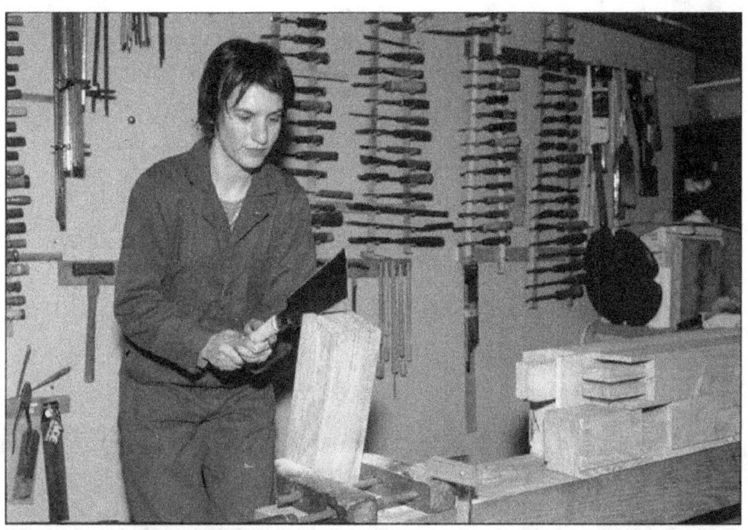

Step eight: Draw the octagonal layout of the leg

Octagon is the best shape for the leg. From the hard cardboard, make an octagonal template and trace it to the bottom end of the legs. Draw the line up the face of the leg, until it is 10.5 inches below the beamline, using a marking gauge. The octagon layout determines the chamfered corners, while the line set with the marking gauge determines the leg final surface. Draw lamb's tongues to not disturb the tenons.

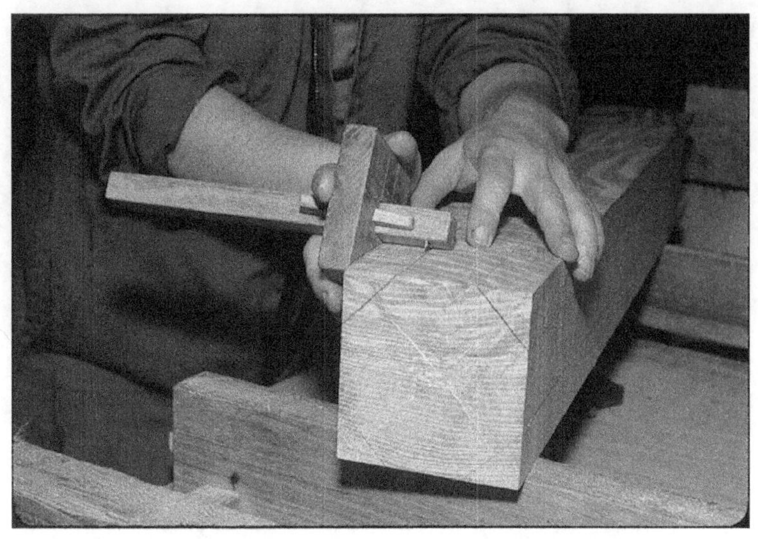

Step nine: Cut the leg corners

Cut out the leg corners marked out above with a hand saw. Also, ensure you fix your eyes on the edges to cut on the marked lines without making any mistakes and cut the leg corners up to the lamb's tongues.

Step 10: Smoothen the final surface

Cutting the legs will give it a rough octagonal shape. Use a drawknife, Japanese hand plane, and chisels to cleanly smoothen the octagonal-shaped legs and lamb's tongue.

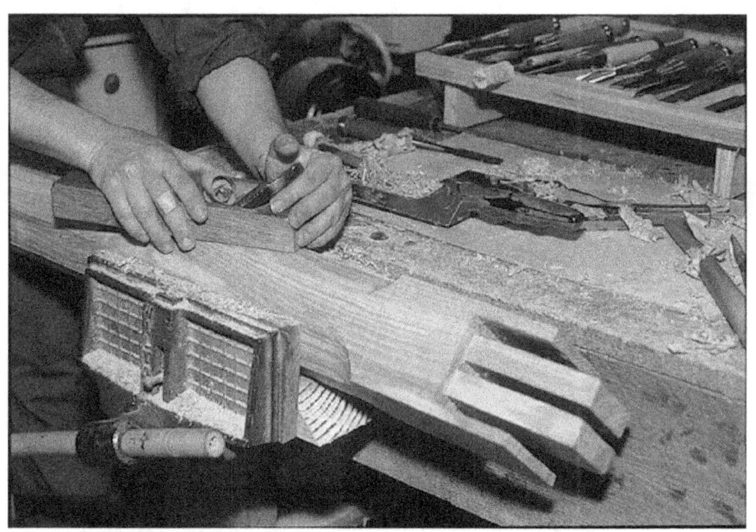

Step 11: Insert the legs

This is the table smackdown stage. The ends of the legs are chamfered to receive the big mallet.

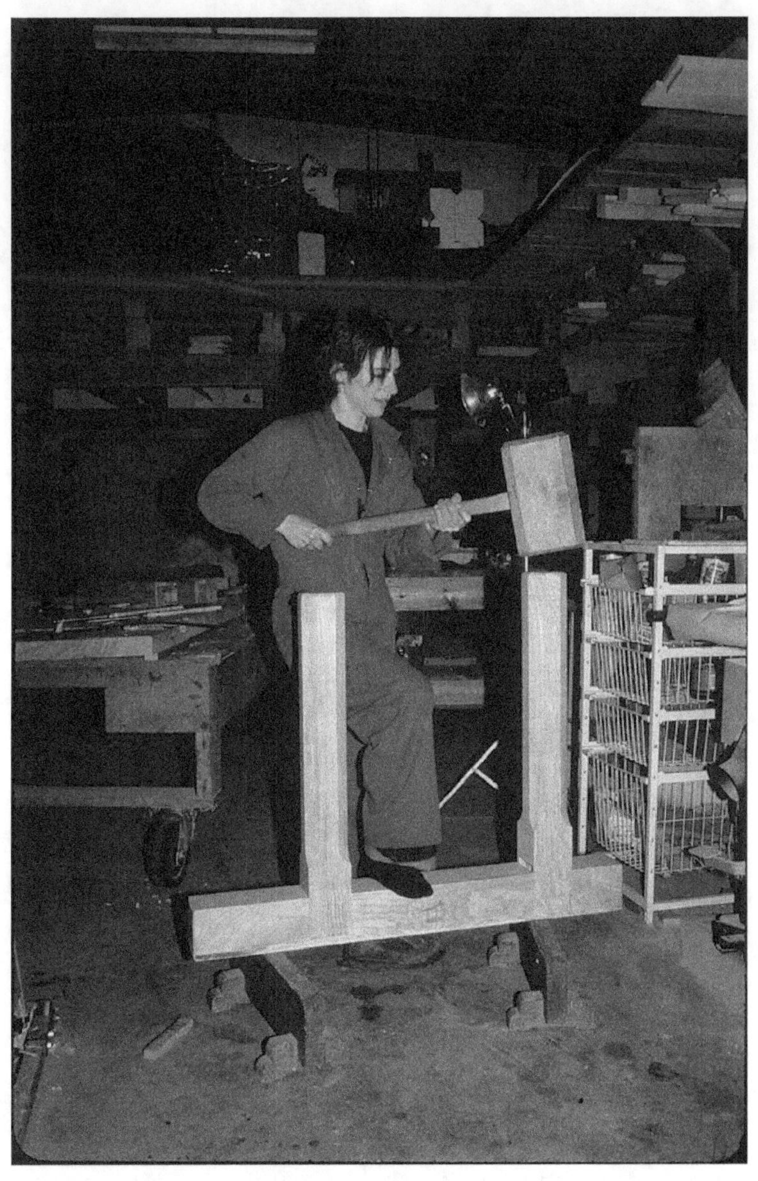

Step 12: Cut a little slit for the wedges

Assemble the mortise and tenon joints with glue and wedges. You should cut a small slit for wedges on the tenon, but remember that the non-shouldered tenons are on the two sides of the center tenons. This makes it hard to use a saw to rip the slits. However, the outside tenons stop at the bottom of the tabletop. So, the center tenons will be longer than the outside tenons. Cut the outside tenons to their actual length, and rip the slits with a small Japanese rip saw. Ensure that all the legs are fitted, and the joints are adjusted, accordingly.

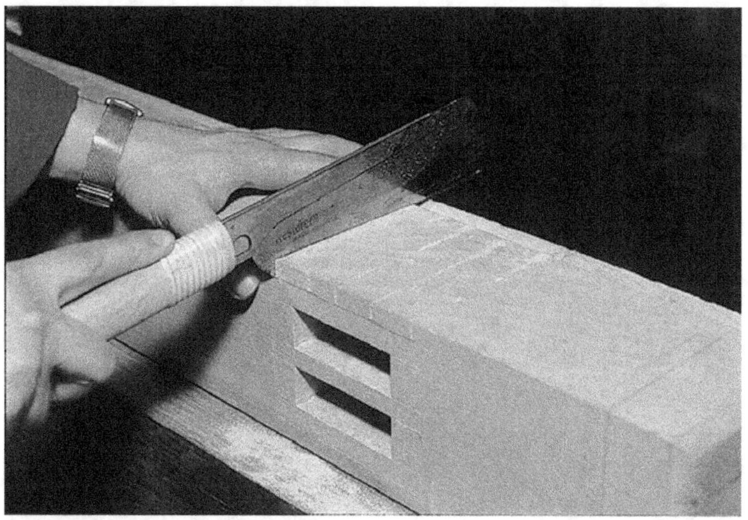

Step 13: Complete the leg-to-beam joint

After cutting and planing every part, use a plane sander to smoothen all the legs, the bottom surface of the table and sliding dovetail beams. Now, you're ready to assemble the legs to the sliding beam using glue. Pound one leg at a time so that the tenons will come out of the beam, fitting tightly.

Hammer and glue the wedges into the slits and leave the leg there to assemble another one. Return to the first leg to cut and plane the tenons flush with the beams. The other leg is finished likewise.

Clean and sand the non-shouldered tenons with a palm sander. Plane the top of the leg's tenon before the final assembly so that the tenons will not touch the tabletop in the future. You can pound the beam into the top for the last time.

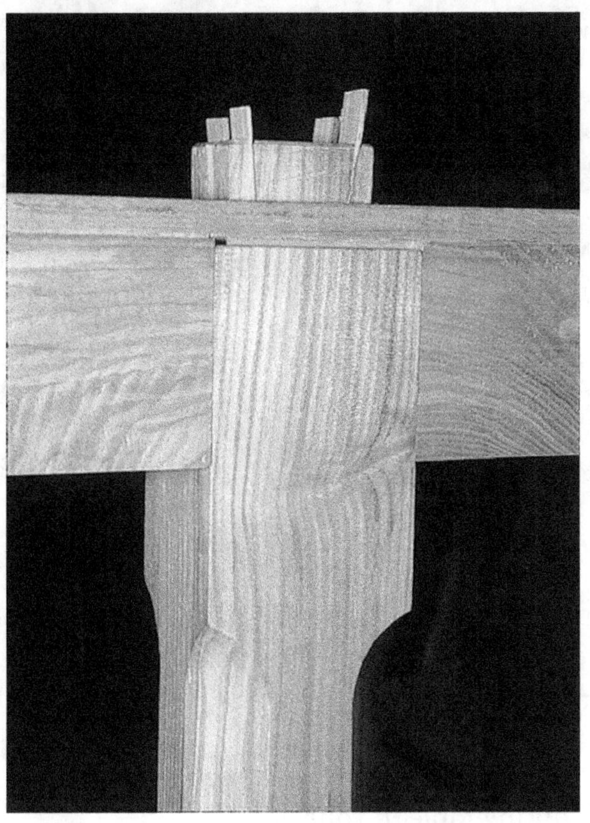

Step 14: Attach the legs and beams

The ends of the beams, together with the attached legs. are pounded, while the legs gradually moved to the center of the table. Finally, the beam mark will eventually come to the edge of the table. You can now measure the length of the legs evenly and cut them with a Japanese saw. The octagon edges should be chamfered and the end grain planted. That's all.

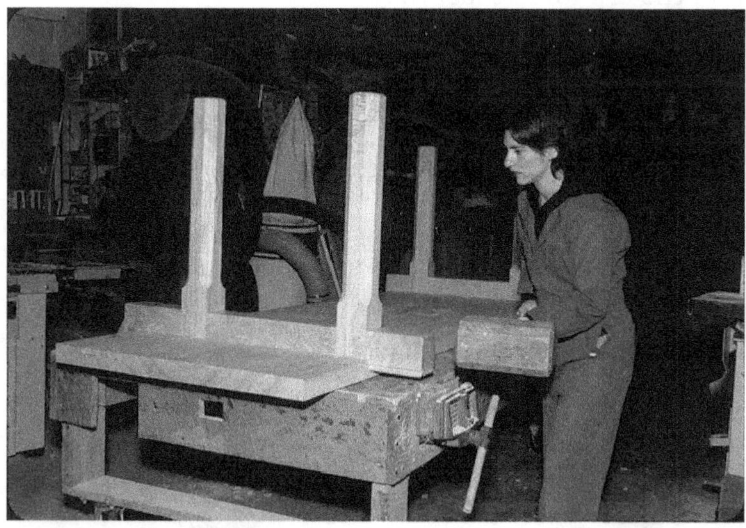

Chapter Summary

One of the most practical chapters of this book—chapter seven—took into consideration the following important subjects:

- The importance of a dining room vis-à-vis a dining table in your house.

- The influence of size, shape, style and space in choosing a dining table.

- Design of the table on paper.

- What joints would make the construction worthwhile?

- The step-by-step procedures for building a dining table.

It's time to look at another concept—lacquering and preservation of wooden objects.

It deals with the meaning, kinds of Japanese lacquering, etc. Chapter 8 promises to be interesting and insightful. So, let's go there.

Chapter Nine: Lacquering and Preserving a Wooden Object

Lacquer is a term used to refer to a range of hard and shiny finishes, which are applied to woods or metals. In modern techniques, it means a number of pigmented or clear coatings that dry through the process of solvent evaporation to yield a sturdy but durable finish.

There is the Japanese lacquerware, which is also known as true lacquer. They're objects coated with the treated, dried and dyed sap of a tree called *Toxicodendron vernicifluum* (the Japanese varnish tree) or any other related tree. This Japanese lacquer—also known as **Urushi**—is applied in many coats to a base that is usually wood. It dries to a very hard and smooth layer, which is strong, beautiful, long-lasting, waterproof and attractive to the eyes.

Permit me to explain here that lacquerware is the art of building artworks and designs using the sap of the Urushi tree. The sap on its own contains one powerful resin known as urushiol. This resin polymerizes under air and moisture to become a hard, durable and plastic-like substance called Japanese lacquer.

When it dries, Japanese lacquer stops the attack of moisture and forms a sturdy film that precludes decay. It's of little wonder that lacquer has been applied on everyday items right from ancient days. In japan, lacquerware items, such as trays, bowls, chopsticks and many-tiered boxes, are easily found there.

They're sometimes painted with pictures, carved, dusted with gold, inlaid with other materials, as well as given other decorative treatments. The techniques used in lacquer have been perfected over many centuries ago so as to produce beautifully detailed designs for furniture, woods, and boxes meant for domestic use.

Kinds of Japanese lacquering

Japanese lacquer differs in quality, color and surface texture. But, lacquer has pigments added to it and traditional pigment colors include black, red, off-white, green and yellow.

The following are the various types of Japanese lacquer (Urushi).

Tame Nuri: It makes use of a clear lacquer that is applied on base material. This allows the elegance of the base material to be very visible.

Tsumakure: It has red accents painted on items. This type of Japanese lacquer is often seen on the edges of *tana*, which literally means *red fingernails.*

Shin Nuri: This type has a smooth and shiny black layer. Multiple coats of lacquer are applied to the wood, sanded and smoothened to achieve this type of lacquer

Tatakinuri: It has a non-shiny but rough texture. This 'pebbly' texture is achieved by mixing different materials into the lacquer, including tofu, crushed eggshells and okara. Okara are small pieces of materials left over in the manufacturing process of tofu. Now, the mixture is applied to the object using a sponge and tapping (tataki) motion. The surface is smoothed using a roller. As a result, this Japanese lacquer type creates a hard surface. It has been applied to Japanese body armor.

Kaki-awase Nuri: This is the lowest grade of black lacquer. A coat of seshime-urushi mixed with lamp-black is applied to the wood, and it hardens the surface of the wood, as well as stains it with black color. This is followed by one good coat of joohana-urushi or joochin-urushi.

How wooden objects are prone to fading, termite and fungal attack

Wooden objects are prone to fading, termite and fungal attack, as well as other problems, based on the kind of wood involved. The truth is the wooden products are subject to deterioration from a number of biological agents such as fungi, termites; physical deterioration such as fading, poor handling, as well as other issues ranging from heat to light and chemical degradation. Let's discuss them one after the other, in three stages.

- **Biological degradation**

Given a favorable condition, a variety of different organisms will attack your wooden object. They include termites, fungi, bacteria, etc. For instance, termites, such as furniture beetles, white and black ants, as well as other insects, cause serious damage to wooden objects, especially softwoods like pines and fir, old furniture made of oak and walnut, and hardwoods.

They're also found in museums, damp timber or in structural timbers of recent buildings. Most of these organisms thrive well in the presence of moisture, limited amount of air and moderate temperatures.

The sapwood and heartwood of most wooden species are prone to attack by a range of various wood rotting and staining fungi. Most of them flourish in dirty, damp, and unventilated environments.

- **Physical degradation**

Wooden objects may be physically damaged by either poor handling or as a result of stresses induced by changing moisture gradients. Its relative softness means that the object can be easily damaged by contact with harder and sharper objects or surfaces.

Excessively hot and dry conditions cause wood objects to shrink and crack. Conversely, cold and damp conditions cause these objects to swell and warp. Substantial damage may be caused by large, rapid fluctuations in relative humidity levels. This is particularly so if wooden parts are closely joined and if their respective grains run contrary to one another. The restriction of free movement often leads to warping and cracking.

The rate of change of relative humidity levels and the way in which the wood has been sawed (along or across the grain, radially) determine whether the wood will become bowed, cupped, twisted, cracked or split as a result of exposure to inappropriate or changing relative humidity conditions.

The expansion and contraction of wood may damage either the wood itself or materials attached to it. Physical damage may occur if no precautions are taken when wooden objects are transported from one climate/region to another. For example, wooden sculptures transported from tropical regions to drier areas commonly develop serious cracks as moisture is lost from the wood. Similar damage may occur if items composed of wood or other organic substances are exposed to hot sunlight during the day and cold, moist conditions at night.

- **Other issues**

Included in this category are thermal (heat), chemical and light. The most drastic form of thermal degradation is the complete damage of wood by heat, fire or burning. Physical damage will happen if a wooden object is placed close to a heat source. The resultant loss of moisture often brings about shrinking and cracking of the wood. Thermal degradation is considered to be the most deadly threat to wood items kept indoors.

Chemical, mechanical and light energy factors combine to contribute to the deterioration of wooden objects that are exposed outdoors to the elements of weather. The general appearance and surface finishes of historic structures are often affected.

When wood is kept reasonably dry and exposed to sunlight or UV radiation, the surface tends to turn brown. A grey finish is observed when the effects of light and moisture are combined. Excessive light exposure will cause bleaching of certain dyes or pigments and fading or discoloration of surface finishes.

Preservation techniques

Rot-inducing fungi can be stopped by removing one of these four elements that make the fungi to live:

- Enough moisture;

- Oxygen;

- Food; and

- **Temperature.**

Only one of these elements needs to be removed to prevent wood decay. The easiest method is to keep the wooden item dry. Most rot-causing fungi will not attack wood if the moisture content is less than 20 percent.

The oxygen component can be removed by submerging the wood in water. Logs that cannot be processed soon after felling and bucking should be placed under a water sprinkler system or submerged in water.

The food component cannot be removed, but it could be poisoned by preservative-treating the wood. Also, temperatures below 50 degrees Fahrenheit will allow negligible fungi growth, and temperatures above 200 degrees Fahrenheit are deadly to fungi.

Handling decay

Since most decay problems are caused by moisture, the solution is quite simple. Eliminate the source of moisture. Check the roof, walls and plumbing for leaks. Go outside and check the eaves and gutters.

Are the eaves wide enough to prevent water from coming down the sidewalls? Are your gutters poorly maintained or missing? Be sure the foundation is not cracked and the soil slopes away from the house. Don't just treat the mildew, mold or decay.

If the decay is too drastic, and you want to preserve the historic or architectural character of moldings, carvings or furniture, consider an epoxy repair job. Epoxies contain resin and hardeners that are mixed just before use.

Liquids for injection and spatula-applied pastes are available. After curing, epoxy-stabilized wood can be shaped with regular woodworking tools and painted. Epoxies are no preservatives and will not stop existing decay. They can be tricky to use, so follow all label directions.

The prevention and control of termites are based on the same factors that affect the growth of wood-destroying fungi as stated above. The best method to prevent attack by termites is to build wooden structures in a manner that allows the wood to be kept dry.

Structural and sanitary measures will not give complete protection against termites, so a chemical means of protection is often the best. The ideal time to install a chemical barrier under a home or shed is at the time of construction. But if a building becomes infested, steps can be taken to dry the wood or construct a chemical barrier between the nest and the infested wooden object.

Also, nests and potential nesting places near the building should be eliminated if they can be found. Contact a reputable pest control company for assistance when termites attack wooden structures.

Preservation treatments

Factory-applied preservatives fall into two general classes: those with an oily nature, such as creosote and petroleum solutions of pentachlorophenol, and those that are dissolved or suspended in water and applied as water solutions. The main difference is the type of liquid used to carry the toxic chemicals into the wood structure.

Heavy oil preservatives have some advantage in extremely wet situations, since besides being toxic to fungi, the liquid carrier slows liquid water movement. A serious drawback to the oil-based treatments is that the wood surface is oily and difficult to finish or paint.

It is possible to use light organic solvents as the carrier for toxic compounds so the wood may be painted after treatment. These solvents evaporate rapidly, leaving the wood with an untreated appearance.

Preventive techniques/conservation

In order to ensure your wooden objects are well-taken care of, take the following factors into account:

- Light, temperature and relative humidity;

- Handling techniques;

- Modes of storage, display and support; and

- Protection from insects, fungi and dirt.

Environmental conditions

To maintain wooden objects in the best condition, the following environmental conditions are ideal and suitable:

- The relative humidity levels should be in the range of 40 to 60 percent, with a maximum variation of 5 percent in any 24-hour period.

- The temperature range of 15 to 25 degrees Centigrade (59 to 77 degrees Fahrenheit) with a maximum variation of 4 degrees Centigrade in any 24-hour period.

- Also, the light levels should be 50 lux for dyed or painted wood, up to 200 lux for undyed or uncoated wood, and a maximum of 300 lux for wooden objects that have largely been used outdoors or have otherwise lost their natural coloring.

- Do not keep wooden objects in direct contact with outside walls or in areas in which large variations in temperature and relative humidity are expected. Avoid keeping wooden objects near fireplaces, heaters, air conditioning vents and doorways. Maintaining relative humidity levels below 65 percent should ensure that fungal attack does not occur.

- In a situation where both metal and wooden components are present in a wooden object, you need to favor one over the other. In these cases, it is preferable to make the conditions more favorable to the wood. This is so because wood is more sensitive to changes in environmental moisture levels than metals.

- Do not expose furniture and other wooden items to direct sunlight. In addition to causing photochemical damage to the wood itself, the joints might be affected, resulting in lifting, shrinkage, warping and cracking.

Handling the objects

Common sense is the best guide when moving or handling any object. Follow the guidelines below:

- Look for assistance when moving large pieces of furniture.

- Always plan ahead. Clear the pathway to and the final location for the object. Ensure you move objects in a slow manner to avoid a fall.

- Hold objects tightly only in areas that can support their full weight, such as the rail of a chair and the apron of a table (not the legs or tabletop).

- Remove any detachable pieces before movement.

- Do not drag the furniture on the floor when moving it. If not, the side thrust on feet or legs can place undue pressure on joints.

- Do not use gloves so as to minimize the risk of dropping wooden objects.

Storage and display of the objects

The following guidelines will help you to properly store, showcase and support wooden objects safely:

- Use stable, inert materials for the construction and support of your wooden items.

- The size of the objects themselves determines the mode of storage. So, drawers, shelves, cupboards or even the floor itself may be right.

- If drawers are used for storage, use enameled metal drawers instead. You can use wooden drawers, but run away from chipboard, as well as other composition boards.

- Store flat. wooden objects on level surfaces. For objects that have irregular surfaces, look for specially constructed supports or padding.

- Padding may be used only if the object's stability is not compromised.

- Big flat-bottomed objects may be stored on the floor but should be raised on padded blocks to allow for even air circulation.

- Use dust covers for covering and keeping furniture clean and free from dust.

- Do not see historic furniture as ordinary furniture as they form part of a collection. For instance, do not sit on the chairs in such a collection.

- Be careful what is placed on a piece of furniture, as sharp objects may scratch the surface, and hot items, condensation or liquid spills can badly affect surface finishes.

- Maintain a stable, clean environment.

- Put bubble wrap and dust covers over large wooden objects.

- Do not keep or consume food and drink very close to the wooden artefacts.

- Inspect objects regularly, looking for signs of insect attack, such as flight holes that may have fallen from such holes.

- Large wooden objects kept outdoors should be kept under cover on a concrete pad to protect them from weathering elements. This will help to stop undue access by black and white ants.

Extra protection from weathering can be achieved by maintaining painted or varnished surfaces. Dust these objects regularly.

- Use stands to raise wheeled objects from the ground. This takes the weight of the vehicle off the wheels and reduces access by ants.

- If transporting wooden objects between regions of differing relative humidity, take precautions to allow the object to acclimatize to its new environment.

Chapter Summary

This chapter discussed everything you need to know about Japanese lacquering. It started with an introduction to the concept and delved into many other areas, such as:

- Kinds of Japanese lacquering.

- How wooden objects are prone to fading, fungi attack, etc.

- The preventive techniques you can take to stop it.

The next item on the list is a ride into Japanese joinery and Taoism—the Zen philosophy. We'll look at the relationship between Japanese joinery and Taoism and how they connect to Japanese spiritual culture. If you're ready, let's go.

Chapter Ten:
Japanese Joinery And Taoism

For many people, the attraction of Japanese joinery is dependent on the fact that it reminds them of the very old world of handcrafts. Though not existing now, it was an era that was in peace with nature through the careful observation of its cycles and rhythms.

In the same vein, it is the aesthetic of the assembly for others, whose technique comes precisely from that observation of the natural rhythms presented by the geometric union, often invisible, of all the parts. The process of interlocking, which joins the wood through self-sustaining joints, was already an extensively used skill. This skill was so much around when the *Miya-Daiku* built their famous Zen temples and teahouses.

Japanese carpentry keeps the singularity of each one of its master craftsmen. It also conserves the spirit of the tree that produced each piece. But all of the changes that happen in the creative process belong to a subtle and discreet world. This is similar to the hidden joints in furniture or houses where what matters is the beauty, strength, and long-lasting quality of the wood used in the construction process.

The invisible assembly seen in the modern world represents the survival of an art form that directly imitates the discretion of nature. It is not the interest in the piece of furniture itself that is important, but what is more important is a good piece that appears to be meditating in place. As you know, a master craftsman would hardly design a plastic chair.

Japanese joinery and woodworking is seen as something that is far more than simply a trade. Many see it as an art form that includes Japanese philosophical knowledge of aesthetics to build strong and excellent products. Japanese craftsmanship is founded on the skill developed to a high degree to which Japanese woodworking is the highest example.

One of the reasons Japanese woodworking and joinery are still relevant and widely used today is as a result of the demand for handmade superlative furniture that has survived the industrialization of the wood and furniture industry.

Also, one of the most attractive and interesting parts of Japanese woodworking is that every joint is compressively held together without screws and glue. The joints are precisely crafted to enable the tightness of the joint in such a way that it doesn't warp or break. Typically, the wood from naturally fallen trees is used to form the foundation of the structure or object to be made.

In the world of traditional Japanese woodworking and joinery, it is uncommon to introduce new methods and technologies within the craft. The introduction of new technologies makes the creative processes lose the human touch, as well as the wood. Rather, most artisans aim to hold fast to the historical methods and techniques within the Japanese joinery art.

To fully understand how Japanese joinery developed alongside its deeply rooted cultural beliefs, one must look back into the history of Japanese Taoism and how it connects to Japanese joinery.

Aesthetic Zen philosophy

The majority of the values seen in the way the Japanese have chosen to create and decorate furniture is traceable to two important religions, namely native Shinto and Chinese-controlled Zen Buddhism, with a particular reference to the tea ceremony.

Shintoism

The most important belief of Shintoism is the worship of kami, the spirits that live in people, places, inanimate objects, such as trees, stones and other natural-existing things. The worship for nature has deep influence on Japanese craftsmen who want to offer trees and even their kami a new life by way of creating nice objects with the wood.

So, the respect Japanese have for trees makes them respect the wood. Lumber is cut for the sole purpose of reducing wastage and maximizing the elegance and character of each wood. Large layers are finished with a mirror polish. Many wood pieces are finished in a way to mark the beauty and grain of the wood, either by using a clear lacquer or leaving the wood unfinished.

Strong joinery is applied to create lasting wooden objects that will preserve the spirit of the tree for a long time. This same reverence for the tree is influenced by Japanese way of not tampering with the natural edge of the boards, whether on the edge of the table or on the surfaces of architectural beams and posts.

Zen, tea ceremony and discipline

The Zen Buddhism and its associated tea ceremony came from China and quickly became a ritual practice among the Japanese elite. As a result of the long Japanese history of taking part in the tea ceremony, the act of deciding how visibly old and decaying things have become a major traditional aesthetic, even outside of the tea house. This results in a love for wooden and furniture objects.

Japanese Zen Buddhism and Chinese Chan Buddhism were attractive to martial groups in the two countries. The tea ceremony reflects this through its styled nature in which every object has its complete form and place. In the same vein, furniture, which is designed to be evocative and mysterious of the spirit of nature, is also built to be absolutely accurate, simple and highly stylized in use.

The discipline needed in Zen Buddhism supported patience and perfectionism. This translated into furniture that is beautiful and looks deceptively simple to build. The complexity, accuracy and precision with which Japanese joinery is built is a distinguishing characteristic of Japanese furniture.

Chapter Summary

As seen in many other components of Japanese culture and tradition, it is the combination of native Shinto ideas and those of Zen Buddhism that weave the excellent tapestry of Japanese woodworking and furniture traditions. So, Japanese joinery has a strong connection to Taoism, and both work to preserve Japanese culture and tradition through woodworking and carpentry.

Final Words

Nowhere is joinery and traditional carpentry more apparent than Japan, a nation with an architectural tradition like no other. Long before screws, nails and metal fastenings became the order of the day, Japanese craftsmen had already become professionals in the art of wood joinery. Using techniques handed down in guilds and families for centuries, Japanese craftsmen, artisans, woodworkers and builders would fit wooden beams together without any external fasteners. Buildings and other wooden objects would stand for generations, held together with nothing more than tension and friction.

Currently, Japan boasts many craftsmen actively engaged in the pursuit of traditional woodworking crafts. The good part of it is that many of them are well-advanced in years. But unfortunately, only a few young Japanese show interest in carrying on these age-long traditions of their fathers.

My hope is that this book will leave you, the reader, with a general understanding of the importance of woodworking with a particular reference to Japanese joinery. With this knowledge, you should be able to make long-lasting projects for your home and keep the Japanese joinery and traditional woodworking craft alive.